W9-CFD-744

THE

CREED

THE
CREED

*Professing the Faith
Through the Ages*

SCOTT HAHN

EMMAUS
ROAD
PUBLISHING

Steubenville, Ohio
www.emmausroad.org

Emmaus Road Publishing
1468 Parkview Circle
Steubenville, Ohio 43952

© 2016 Scott Hahn
All rights reserved. Published 2016
Printed in the United States of America

Library of Congress Control Number: 2016936213
ISBN: 978-1-941447-77-2

Cover design and layout by Margaret Ryland

To our newest beloved grandchildren:

Adrian Scott Marie Hahn
Theresa Catherine Reinhard
Francesca Chiara Hahn
Joseph Pio Hahn

TABLE OF CONTENTS

CHAPTER 1 The Creed Makes Us 1

CHAPTER 2 The Need for Creed: The Old Testament
Prehistory of the New Testament Profession 15

CHAPTER 3 A New Covenant and a New Confession...25

CHAPTER 4 The Thundering Kanon 35

CHAPTER 5 From Freedom to Formula..........................45

CHAPTER 6 The Crown of the Council..........................55

CHAPTER 7 The Setting of the Creed...........................67

CHAPTER 8 Points of Light..75

CHAPTER 9 Father Forever 85

CHAPTER 10 The Creator of All....................................99

CHAPTER 11 Son Worship 109

CHAPTER 12 That's the Spirit...................................... 127

CHAPTER 13 The Church and the Future.................... 141

CHAPTER 14 Amen 157

APPENDIX A: Important Later Creeds 163

APPENDIX B: A Biblical Creed 183

SELECTED BIBLIOGRAPHY 187

CHAPTER I

THE CREED MAKES US

Singer-songwriter Rich Mullins earned lasting fame with a series of contemporary Christian hits in the 1980s and 1990s. In less than a decade, he won a dozen Dove Awards. His anthem "Awesome God" remains a staple of evangelical praise. Mullins' early music was influenced by his Quaker upbringing, which was austerely anti-dogmatic, and his "Independent Christian" young adulthood. The Bible college he attended grew out of a movement whose foundational slogans touted "No creed but Christ."

Reading in Christian history, he was attracted to the figure of St. Francis of Assisi, a fellow poet given to spontaneous praise, a lover of spiritual freedom. Yet, as Mullins learned, Francis drew his poetry from a deep well of Catholic doctrine and liturgy—from a tradition crystallized in creeds.

Mullins' study led him to love the creeds, so much, in fact, that he enrolled himself into RCIA classes at a Catholic parish in 1997. He died in an automobile accident that September, on the very eve of the day he was to be received into full communion with the Catholic Church. The music he produced in that home stretch shows the change in his interior life. Among his most mature works is the song "Creed," with its mighty chorus:

> *And I believe what I believe*
> *is what makes me what I am.*
> *I did not make it. No, it is making me.*
> *It is the very truth of God and not*
> *the invention of any man.*
> *I believe it, I believe.*

What was true for Rich Mullins is true for you and me as well. What we believe is making us what we are—and what we hope to be for all eternity. It is a grace from God. You and I and Rich Mullins and St. Francis have been pleased to pledge it, to confess it, in the Church's creeds.

◆ ◆ ◆

A creed is an authoritative summary of Christianity's basic beliefs. In the articles of the creed, we profess our faith in mysteries—doctrines that could never be known apart from divine Revelation: that God is a Trinity of persons, that God the Son took flesh and was born of a virgin, and so on. If God had not revealed the mysteries of Christianity, the mysteries we rehearse in the creed, we could never have figured them out on our own.

A creed is *not* the totality of Christian faith. It's a

summary that stands for everything that is taught by the Catholic Church, which is itself one of the mysteries we proclaim in the creed. A creed is a symbol of something larger—and, ultimately, of Someone we love, Someone who makes us who we are, by means of creeds and other graces.

The Catechism of the Catholic Church puts it eloquently when it says that we do not believe in formulas, but in the *realities* expressed by those formulas, which faith allows us to touch (see CCC 170). Faith is our *personal* clinging to God and to his truth in its entirety (see CCC 150). It is our act of trust in everything God is and says and asks of us. Our object is not a proposition, but a Person. Yet we cannot love someone whom we do not know. The propositions of the creed help us along the way of knowledge, which is our way to love.

◆ ◆ ◆

The word "creed" comes from the Latin word *credo*—literally translated: "I believe!" That is the phrase with which Christians have usually begun their professions of faith. As we'll see, there is strong evidence that such summary acts of faith have been integral to Christianity from the very start. *Credo* (or its Aramaic equivalent) is the word cried out by the desperate father who begs Jesus for the healing of his child: "I believe; help my unbelief!" (Mk 9:24). It is the word of the man blind from birth, whom Jesus healed—it is the word that serves as a prelude to true worship (Jn 9:38). *Credo* is also the cry of grieving Martha; it is the word Jesus deliberately draws from her before he raises her brother Lazarus (Jn 11:27).

St. Paul seems to allude to creedal statements when he says: "If you confess with your lips that *Jesus is Lord* and believe in your heart that God raised him from the dead, you will be saved. For man believes with his heart and so is justified, and he confesses with his lips and so is saved" (Rom 10:9–10).

In the ordinary course of love, we believe with our heart and confess with our lips. If we live with integrity, there is a unity of our thoughts, words, and deeds—our hearts and hands and voices. We say what we mean, and we do as we say. We "walk the talk."

This doesn't mean, however, that our recitation of the creed presumes a mastery of material. As Rich Mullins put it, the creed "is making" us. That "making" is an ongoing process. Think again about that desperate father in the Gospel. He shouted out to Jesus, "I believe," but then he quickly added, "Help my unbelief!" (Mk 9:24).

A creed marks the way of conversion for a pilgrim Church on earth and for each of its members.

◆ ◆ ◆

Thus, creeds have always been an important part of the Rite of Baptism. This was one way the early Church made sure to fulfill Jesus' command: "Go therefore and make disciples of all nations, baptizing them in the name of the Father and of the Son and of the Holy Spirit" (Mt 28:19). Some of the most ancient creeds we know are simple statements professing belief in each of the Persons of the Blessed Trinity. If they elaborate at all, they add statements affirming that Jesus is both God and man, that he founded a Church, and that the dead will be raised.

In the Church's beginning, there were no Bibles, no missals, no hymnals. The Apostles would summarize the saving events of Jesus' life, often in short, skeletal sermons—summaries of the Gospel—that came to be known as the "rule of faith." In chapter 2 of the Acts of the Apostles, we see this process at work. Peter preached a summary of Christ's life and mission (see especially 2:29–36). The people experienced a change of heart (v. 37) and "received his word" and "were baptized" (v. 41) and went on to receive the Eucharist (v. 42).

The creed was their gateway to the graced transformation made possible by the sacraments of initiation.

We find this pattern repeated frequently in the New Testament and, afterward, in the works of the early Church Fathers.

The rule of faith took many forms, but it always proclaimed certain mysteries: God is one; God became man in Jesus Christ; Christ has died; Christ is risen; Christ is glorified and will come again. Over time, these proclamations became more detailed and more standardized. They were universally recognized marks of faith. In the East, they were known as "measuring sticks."

From early on, there were two general types of creeds: the question-and-answer kind and the declaration kind. We still know both forms today.

The Church uses the Q&A form in Baptisms and at the Easter Vigil. It expresses the movement of conversion in dramatic terms as it moves from a rejection of sin and evil ("Do you reject Satan?" "I do.") to an affirmation of the true God ("Do you believe in God the Father Almighty?" "I do.").

Each "I do" resounds with power and glory and strength of commitment, reminding us of marriage vows and solemn oaths sworn in courtrooms. Like marriage, the creed indeed changes us. It marks a key moment in the story of our ongoing conversion. It *is making* us.

◆ ◆ ◆

The "declaration creed" is even more familiar to us. We recite one of them at every Sunday Mass, and they are made up of a series of sentences that declare our belief in many individual (but interrelated) mysteries: God's fatherhood, Jesus' divine sonship, the Holy Spirit's divinity, the Church's mission.

Most missals give us both the *Nicene Creed* and the *Apostles' Creed*. The Nicene Creed is based upon the faith expressed at the first two ecumenical councils of the Church, the fourth-century Councils of Nicaea (AD 325) and Constantinople (AD 381). The Apostles' Creed is significantly shorter and less detailed; it is based upon the most ancient formula used by the Church in Rome, and we find it in various forms dating back to the 200s.

For the last thousand years, we in the Western churches have normally recited the Nicene Creed during Sunday Masses. The shorter and simpler Apostles' Creed is a suitable substitute for children's Masses.

We recite the creed after the homily. We recite it while standing. It is our custom to bow as we say the words, "And by the Holy Spirit was incarnate of the Virgin Mary, and became man."

The creed is the capstone of the liturgy of the Word. We have heard the words of the prophets and sung the praises of the Psalms. We have received the Gospel as truly as St. Peter's congregation did on that first Pentecost. Now, as we recite the creed, we say our "yes," our *Credo*, like that of the pleading father in the Gospel, like that of the man blind from birth, like that of Martha. We raise up what we have received.

It's significant that, in our liturgy, the creed follows after the Bible readings, since the creed is a summary of the history of salvation. It's helpful, too, that it comes after the homily. So even if our pastor is having a bad day and his sermon notes don't quite come together, we always end well with the Rule of Faith.

◆ ◆ ◆

Our creeds emerged from those simplest and most ancient forms, but they developed over time. As the Church faced misunderstandings, dissensions, and threats, it became necessary to respond with ever-clearer teaching. The Church's doctrine did not (and does not) supersede the words of Scripture. Dogma is, rather, the Church's infallible reflection on Scripture. For the Bible is not a self-interpreting text. The Bible itself says so!

Think of the time in the Acts of the Apostles when St. Philip sees the Ethiopian man reading Isaiah the prophet. Philip asks him, "Do you understand what you are reading?" And the man says, "How can I, unless someone guides me?" Philip responds by preaching the Rule of Faith (Acts 8:31).

Two thousand years later we are not so technologically advanced that we no longer need such assistance.

Christians certainly needed it in the fourth century, when some people began to claim that Jesus was not "God" in the same way as the Father was God. Jesus was not, they said, coeternal and coequal with the Father. This movement—called Arianism after the name of its most famous proponent—spread rapidly through the Church. A few decades later another movement threatened the traditional Christian faith in the divinity of the Holy Spirit.

To counter such opposition the Church gathered in councils and forged the more detailed creeds. They had to do it, for the stakes were high. What was under attack was the truth about God—the truth about our salvation. And the heretics made persuasive arguments "proving" their false doctrine from the pages of Scripture. History was making it clear that there were true and false ways of reading the Bible. The Arians and the Catholics held doctrines that were mutually exclusive. One had to be right and the other wrong.

The councils pointed out that the heretics could not square their interpretation with the way Christians had always understood the Bible—the way that had been proclaimed throughout the world in the Rule of Faith, the liturgy of Baptism and the Mass, and the earliest creeds.

◆ ◆ ◆

At the Council of Nicaea, the Church employed in its creed a word that did not appear in the Bible. In Greek it is *homoousion*. We translate it to English as "consubstantial." But even though the term is not in Scripture, it sums up the very meaning of Scripture.

Homoousion captures the basic meaning of sonship. We know from our earthly families that children—sons or daughters—must share the nature of their parents. A human father cannot sire a puppy or a kitten; nor can he adopt one as his legally recognized offspring.

When we say that Christ is "consubstantial with the Father," we are saying that he is God as the Father is God. They are coeternal. They are coequal. They share a love that is life-giving, a love we know in an analogous and imperfect way through human fatherhood.

Through the Incarnation, God the Son became what we are. He stooped down to the level of a creature, taking up what is ours and giving us what is his. He didn't just assume human nature to wear it, like a jersey or a jacket, for a day or two. He lived human life concretely and in the most painful and sacrificial ways. The life he lived is a revelation of sonship, and that sonship is a revelation of God's *eternal* fatherhood. God the Father is the perfect Father, and there was never a time when he was not a Father, for he always dwelt with the Son in the uniting love of the Holy Spirit.

Jesus became what we are so that we might become what he is. Through Baptism we have become "partakers of the divine nature" (2 Pet 1:4). From that moment, we dwell in Christ and he dwells in us. Sharing his nature, we share his sonship. We live the love of the Trinity.

That is our baptismal faith. It is the faith we profess in our baptismal creeds. To profess a different belief is to believe in a different God and to hope for a different salvation. But there is no other God, and there is no other salvation.

The great Fathers of the fourth century knew that, and they were willing to give their lives rather than change the articles of the creed. Their opponents—those who wished for a compromise with the heretics—proposed a least-common-denominator approach to doctrine. They suggested that a single letter be added to *homoousion*— the Greek letter *iota*, which would change its meaning from "one in being" to "similar in being." It was a catch-all phrase, because objects that were one and the same could also, and truthfully, be called "similar." But the Fathers would not accept this watering down of the faith and the councils explicitly rejected it. One *iota* made all the difference in the world. Some Christians were martyred because of that little letter.

The creed, as it has come down to us, conveys the relational core of Christian faith. In telling the truth about the Father, Son, and Holy Spirit, we profess that the mystery of God is the interpersonal relations we are called to share. We proclaim the relationship for which we have been reborn, and by which we are empowered to live as Jesus lived, to die with Jesus, and to rise again to everlasting life.

And so, in the words of the Church, we "renew" our baptismal covenant with the words of the creed. And we are renewed. We are made a new creation, proceeding from glory to glory (2 Cor 3:18).

By God's grace, the creed is making us.

◆ ◆ ◆

This book is an introduction to the creed. By "creed" I mean not any particular statement; for the Church has produced many. I will focus on the creed produced by the fourth-century councils at Nicaea (AD 325) and Constantinople (AD 380), simply because it is well developed and accepted by a wide variety of Christians.

In the early chapters, however, I want to trace the use of creeds in biblical religion, not just in the period of the

New Testament, but long before, in the history of Israel. I want to show that creeds don't just make *you* who *you* are and *I* who *I* am; they also make *us* who *we* are. They are one of the ordinary means God uses to unite his people. God takes wayward tribes and makes them a nation—and, more than that, a family! He takes all the lawless, rebellious nations of the earth and makes of them a Church—and, more than that, his own body! It begins with that cry from the heart: *I believe!*

In the later chapters I want to examine the content of the creed. We hear it so often. We know it by rote. Its language is somewhat abstract. So it's easy for us to miss the revolutionary implications of what we're saying. There are reasons why the Judeans, Romans, and Persians—and so many others—have seen the Christian creed as a threat to the established social order. The creed threatens us all because it promises to make us new—to remake us in the image of Christ—and to fashion us for heavenly life even as we live out our earthly days. The creed captures the momentum of God's original intention at the first moment of creation. Its words are our pure consent.

As we explore the individual articles of the creed, and even drill down into the deeper meaning of small phrases, we'll draw from history, theology, catechesis, the Fathers, the Doctors, the Popes, and the ordinary Magisterium of the Church. But all of that is secondary. What I hope to recover and convey is the creed's revolutionary character. What I want us to remember is the quality of the creed that makes ordinary Christians willing to die to protect a single jot, an *iota*.

What I want is for the creed to make us as it has always made saints. It is Christ who draws us together in these pages—and in that blessed communion that the creed declares. As we know from the Scriptures, the creed itself is our most natural and supernatural response to his Word.

CHAPTER 2

THE NEED FOR CREED:
THE OLD TESTAMENT PREHISTORY OF
THE NEW TESTAMENT PROFESSION

Samson Raphael Hirsch was a rabbi of great learning
and stature. His life spanned much of the nineteenth century (1808–1888). He is considered one of the founders
of the modern Orthodox movement in Judaism. In Ger-
many he served as chief rabbi in several urban centers,
but his influence extended far abroad. He opposed the
liberalizing trends of his time—the emerging movements
of Reform and Conservative Judaism—and he advocated
instead a renewed focus on the observance of the Law of
Moses.

Some of his followers believed that Jews of their time
would benefit from a simple summary of religious tenets.
But both Hirsch and his adversaries resisted the setting of
any fixed formulas. "Deeds, not creeds" was their watch-
word in the English-speaking world. When people asked
Rabbi Hirsch why Jews had no catechism or creed, he re-

sponded: "The catechism of the Jew consists of his calendar."[1]

And there's something to that. The feasts and fasts of biblical religion are a powerful delivery system for basic doctrine. History seems to indicate that Jews and Christians learn their faith most effectively through ritual celebration and remembrance.

Yet there seems also to be a need to codify the basics. In the twelfth century, the rabbi Maimonides made a creedal statement of thirteen principles of faith. Each principle begins with the phrase "I believe with perfect faith . . ." and they cover a range of doctrinal principles: the oneness and uniqueness of the Creator, his non-physicality, the efficacy of prayer, the truth of Scripture, the authority of the Law, the expectation of the Messiah, and so on.

Maimonides met with limited success. Though some congregations adopted his formula, others opposed it—vehemently—for its inclusions and its omissions. Half a millennium later, the idea of a creed for Jews seemed a non-starter with rabbis, whether Orthodox or Reform.

Scholars today, however, look into the Torah—the first five books of the Bible—and into the prophets and other writings, and they find that ancient Israel *indeed* had a creed. Recurring in the Scriptures of our Old Testament is a bare-bones summary of doctrine that set the

---

[1] Samson Raphael Hirsch, *Collected Writings, Volume II: The Jewish Year, Part Two* (Nanuet: Feldheim, 1997), 41.

Chosen People apart from all the religions of their neighbor nations.

Israel's confession of faith is the *Shema Yisrael.* The Hebrew title comes from the opening words of the confession, which itself comes verbatim from the exhortation of Moses:

Hear, O Israel: The LORD our God is one LORD; and you shall love the LORD your God with all your heart, and with all your soul, and with all your might.

— Deuteronomy 6:4–5

It is familiar to Christians because it is quoted twice in the Gospels, once by Jesus (Mk 12:29) and once by a lawyer questioning Jesus (Lk 10:27). In the latter instance, it serves as the setup for Jesus' parable of the Good Samaritan.

For Jesus and his contemporaries, the Shema was a touchstone of identity for religious Jews. According to the first-century Jewish historian Josephus, observant Jews recited the prayer twice daily, when they woke up and when they went to bed, reading it from a text they bore with them at all times.[2] To hold the text of the Shema, Jews wore *tefillin,* or phylacteries: small containers usually made of leather (see Mt 23:5). It was customary also to inscribe the first words of the Shema on the door-

---

[2] Josephus, *Antiquities of the Jews* 4.8.13.

post at home and on the gates of Jewish towns and cities. First-century *tefillin*, bearing the Shema, were found among the Dead Sea Scrolls at Qumran.

Eventually the text of the Shema, especially as it was recited in synagogues, was expanded to include other passages from the Torah: Deuteronomy 6:6–9 and 11:13–21 and Numbers 15:37–41. These latter verses serve as a reminder of the commandments and the rewards (blessings) bestowed on anyone who keeps the Law.

The practices related to the Shema were expounded by the great rabbis whose teachings are preserved in the Mishna and Talmud—including St. Paul's original master, Gamaliel.

The Shema was foundational to the religious vocabulary of Jesus' times—and to that of Jews before and afterward. Though it makes no personal statement of faith, no "I believe," it has doctrinal content. It has creedal qualities. But is it a creed? And, if it is, what does it profess or confess?

♦ ♦ ♦

"Form critics" are scholars who study the literary genres of biblical books and passages. They routinely place the Shema, along with other proto-creeds, in the category of "confessions of faith."[3] Such confessions have "both a cognitive truth-claiming content ('that there is no God but

---

3   See, for example, Vernon H. Neufeld, *The Earliest Christian Confessions* (Grand Rapids: Eerdmans, 1963), 34–41.

One') and a self-involving personal stake"[4] in a particular "world."

The Shema certainly qualifies. Yes, it lacks an "I believe" prefatory phrase, but demanding one would be anachronistic. The "I believe" form seems to have emerged only much later, with the early Christian baptismal formulas. In any event, "I believe" is implied in the message of the Shema. Someone who truthfully says "The LORD our God is one" must first believe that the Lord is one and divine. Someone who truthfully continues the recitation of the Shema must also believe that the one God desires the exclusive, loving devotion of every individual member of his Chosen People. Again, that implies something about God: that he is engaged in history and in individual lives, and that he is looking for love.

This "cognitive truth-claiming content" set Israel far apart from its Gentile neighbors, almost all of whom believed in the coexistence and conflict of many divine beings—many "gods." Gentiles offered sacrifice to each god or goddess in turn, and the gods, as a rule, did not demand exclusive attention. Love between a god and a human was not possible. The idea of a divinely sanctioned moral law was also a novelty in the religions of antiquity. The gods neither imposed nor observed laws.

Occasionally, Gentiles reasoned their way to monotheism—to the existence of one supreme god and creator.

---

[4] Anthony C. Thiselton, *The First Epistle to the Corinthians: A Commentary on the Greek Text* (Grand Rapids: Eerdmans, 2000), 630.

(The Egyptian Pharaoh Amenhotep IV, Akhenaten, is the best-known instance.) But these rarely amounted to more than thought experiments, abstract and idiosyncratic. They didn't take hold. As "religions" they were largely confined to their authors and died when the authors died.

The Shema bespeaks a religion far different—a God who makes himself known, and makes demands, and whose dominion is universal, and who rewards and punishes human behavior, and lives in love with his people.

It involves, moreover, a personal stake in the history of the Lord God's relations with the world he created. To recite the Shema—as to recite any confession coined by Jews or Christians—is to place oneself squarely within that history. It is to claim a place with a particular people.

In the religion of Israel, all history tells of the particular relationship of the Lord God with his people. The Scriptures describe that relationship with the Hebrew word *b'rith*—covenant. And so covenant is the necessary context for understanding the earliest biblical confession, the proto-creed we know as the Shema.

◆ ◆ ◆

In the Old Testament, the bond between God and his people was described as a "covenant." Covenant is key to understanding the Bible, which is itself divided into the "Old Covenant" and the "New Covenant." (The Hebrew word for covenant, *b'rith*, and the Greek, *diatheke*, are usually translated into English as "Testament.") At the

Last Supper, Jesus identifies Christianity's defining ritual act, the Eucharist, as "the new covenant in my blood" (Lk 22:20). In the words of Old Testament scholar Walter Bruggemann, "Biblical faith is essentially covenantal in its perception of all reality."[5]

That's not a modern discovery. In the second century, St. Irenaeus of Lyon taught that "covenant" defines the biblical account of human history. To understand "the divine program and economy for the salvation of humanity," it is necessary for us first to understand God's "several covenants with humanity" and also "the special character of each covenant."[6]

What is a covenant relationship? It is a family bond. Frank Moore Cross of Harvard described covenant as the "legal means by which the duties and privileges of kinship may be extended to another individual or group, including aliens."[7] Covenant, then, creates a family bond where none had previously existed. Two examples familiar to modern readers would be marriage and adoption.

In his "several covenants with humanity," God has tried to bring us into communion with him—so that we can live a life that is not only good, but divine. He has perpetually been faithful. His human creatures have perennially failed in holding up their (our) end of the covenant.

---

[5] Walter Bruggemann, "The Covenanted Family," *Journal of Current Social Issues* 14 (1977): 18.

[6] Irenaeus, *Against Heresies* 1.10.3.

[7] F. M. Cross, "Kinship and Covenant in Ancient Israel," in *From Epic to Canon: History and Literature in Ancient Israel* (Baltimore: Johns Hopkins University Press, 1998), 8.

In the ancient world, two parties entered into a covenant by means of an oath invoking God as witness. Then the new bond would be ratified and sealed by the offering of a sacrifice and the sharing of a ritual meal. We see this in the Old Testament accounts of the covenants of Abraham and Moses (for example).

Every covenant imposed obligations on the parties involved. Fulfillment of these requirements brought about blessings and rewards. Failure to fulfill them brought curses and punishments. Nowhere is this stated as starkly as in the Book of Deuteronomy. At the giving of the Law, Moses speaks to the people of "the blessing and the curse, which I have set before you" (Dt 30:1). And he concludes: "I have set before you life and death, blessing and curse; therefore choose life, that you and your descendants may live" (30:19).

Whenever the people of Israel renewed their covenant with God, they reminded themselves of these terms. Any confession of God's existence and action implied an acceptance of the terms of the covenant. Appropriately, such renewals often took the form of a vow or an oath.[8] To declare the truth about God was to insert oneself into the story of Israel—the story of the covenant.

Declarations of covenant renewal were typically stated aloud. The verb used to denote this action is usually rendered in English as "confess" or "confess with your lips." Greek-speaking Jews used the word *homologia*, which was

---

[8] See the discussion in Neufeld, 14–15.

adopted by the early Christians for use with their statements of faith.

The Shema functioned as such a confession, reminding the Chosen People—twice daily—of the true doctrine of God, as revealed to Moses. In its longer form, the Shema also reminded them of the covenant with Israel and its blessings and curses.

Throughout antiquity the Jews invoked this basic statement with a kind of shorthand. They would simply say, "God is one."[9] Those few words would stand as a symbol, representative of the entire truth, the entire covenant, with all of its law and life and sacrificial worship.

All words are symbols; they stand for persons, places, things, actions, and qualities. Words about God strive to do more than ordinary words can do. They strive for the impossible: to represent God in his infinite power, utter simplicity, and unfathomable mystery.

Yet life in love with God seems to demand such striving. We cannot love someone we do not know, and one way God reveals himself is through words. The Shema recognizes that the essence of the covenant is love. God elicits love from his people, in both deeds of the law and creeds of confession.

That is a truth as old as the covenant. It formed the Chosen People, and it made them one. It gave them their identity and an ordering principle for all of life. It makes them who they are.

---

[9] See Neufeld, 36–37.

As a confession of faith in God, it is a shadow of the powerful acclamations to come—in the dispensation of the New Covenant.

CHAPTER 3

A NEW COVENANT AND A NEW CONFESSION

No one needs to profess faith in obvious facts. The playwright Eugene Ionesco demonstrates this in his play *The Bald Soprano*. When his characters make solemn pronouncements about trivial matters—"The ceiling is above; the floor is below"—the effect is absurdly comic. They look silly. The audience is supposed to laugh.

The content of such a line isn't nonsense. But it's nonsense to suppose that anyone would proclaim it or even bother to mention it. We *observe* the relative position of the floor or ceiling. We don't *confess* it. Confessional statements are solemn because they express an interior act of faith in something supremely important—something essential, yet unknowable (or very difficult to know) apart from divine Revelation. We confess our faith in "things that are unseen" and "eternal" (2 Cor 4:18).

So the Jews, in the Shema, confessed God's unicity and their own special election. The cognitive content of the Shema was not self-evident to the Gentiles, who worshipped many gods and held no special regard for Israel. The Shema contained the beliefs that set Israel apart from all others, the tenets that defined them.

The first Christians were Jews. They lived in the same pagan milieu as their ancestors—so they were constrained to make the same basic confession as their ancestors. Thus the affirmation at the heart of the Shema—that "God is one"—appears repeatedly in the New Testament (see, for example, Romans 3:30; Galatians 3:20; and James 2:19). Yet Christians found it necessary to make further distinctions. They needed to distinguish their own beliefs not only from pagan idolaters, but also from Jews who did not recognize Jesus as divine or as the Messiah (the Anointed Redeemer).

In the Gospels we find the Apostles stepping forward to make such acts of faith. Jesus asks Peter, "But who do you say that I am?" And Peter replies: "You are the Christ" (Mk 8:29). This is not something that "flesh and blood" could have reasoned out; it is not a fact Peter could have deduced simply from sensory data. Jesus' status as Messiah is "revealed" to Peter by God in heaven (Mt 16:17). Peter responds with a confession of faith.

Similarly, Thomas sees Jesus risen from the dead and confesses: "My Lord and my God!" (Jn 20:28). He bases his affirmation on what he has seen, but he affirms far more than the empirical data. He identifies Jesus as divine—as God. Jesus responds by emphasizing the "unseen" character of the object of faith: "Have you believed because you have seen me? Blessed are those who have not seen and yet believe" (Jn 10:29).

The confessions of Peter and Thomas seem to represent fairly standard acts of faith from the first generation of Christians. St. Paul, in his Letter to the Romans, spoke of Christian confession in the same terms: "If you confess with your lips that Jesus is Lord and believe in your heart that God raised him from the dead, you will be saved" (Rom 10:9). Paul assumes that a true Christian statement of faith will acknowledge doctrines that set Christianity apart from every other religion: Jesus' divinity, his identity as Messiah, and his Resurrection. He also specifies that a Christian confession should be made *aloud*. Belief may begin "in your heart," but it must also find expression "with your lips." Such a confession, like the Shema before it, marks a covenant with consequences—with blessings and curses, some stated and others implied. *If you make the confession*, Paul emphasizes, *you will be saved*.

Elsewhere we see that the content of the confession was something given to an individual and actively "received" (1 Cor 15:1). The individual believer then confirmed this doctrine aloud as they made "the good confession in the presence of many witnesses" (1 Tim 6:12).

These circumstances seem to correspond to what we know about the Rite of Baptism in the primitive Church. Before the ritual immersion, the basic doctrine of the faith was given to the candidate, who confirmed it by confession in the midst of the community.

The very word we use is a witness to the communal quality of these pre-creedal formulas. Confession derives from two Latin terms that mean "to acknowledge . . . together." The original Greek term, *homologia*, is another compound, and its components mean "words of the same kind"—the words the community holds in common.

The early confessions were declarations of covenant commitment, given individually, but belonging to the whole assembly of the Church. The confessions shaped the lives of the individuals, conforming them to the life of Jesus Christ.

◆ ◆ ◆

In Jesus Christ "the Word became flesh" (Jn 1:14). The fourth Gospel begins with a series of doctrinal statements arranged poetically. The culmination of this prologue is the statement of God's enfleshment, his Incarnation. Since Jesus is the fullness of God's self-revelation, the mission of the Apostles was to bring him to the world.

The Apostles presented "the Word" to the world by means of miracles and deeds, but also—and perhaps especially—by verbal forms. We can say "especially" not because the words are more important than the deeds or rites, but because we know the deeds and rites largely because of their documentary record and the oral transmission of the story. We know the deeds almost entirely by means of words.

The Apostles proclaimed Jesus, taught Jesus, preached Jesus, remembered Jesus, and confessed Jesus through a variety of verbal forms. The Greek words for these forms are rich: *euangelion, leitourgia, kerygma, didache, martyria, paradosis,* and *homologia.* Their English equivalents have become technical terms in Christianity's religious vocabulary: *gospel, liturgy, preaching, doctrine, witness, tradition,* and *confession.* All of these (both the terms and the forms) can be found in the texts of the New Testament. All of them have doctrinal content. All of them feed, in some ways, into the development of the Church's creeds.

These forms do not fall into watertight categories. Indeed, they often overlap. Confessions of faith may appear as stand-alone declarations, but they can also appear in the midst of other forms. Consider the formula most often cited as an example of an early Christian statement of faith: "Jesus is Lord." St. Paul uses it in three different letters: Romans (10:9), First Corinthians (12:3), and (with the addition of the title "Christ") in Philippians (2:11). In Romans he presents the simple confession as the content of his preaching. In his Letter to the Philippians, however, he envisions the proclamation as an act of ritual public worship—liturgy. In First Corinthians the sentence appears as a personal prayer or perhaps a public witness.

In other New Testament passages we find more detailed and developed confessional passages. In these we begin to recognize the phraseology that would one day find its place in the Church's creeds.

> [T]here is one God, the Father, from whom are all things and for whom we exist, and one Lord, Jesus Christ, through whom are all things and through whom we exist.
>
> —1 Corinthians 8:6

> [I]n him all things were created, in heaven and on earth, visible and invisible.
>
> —Colossians 1:16

> Christ died for our sins . . . he was buried . . . he was raised on the third day in accordance with the scriptures.
>
> —1 Corinthians 15:3–4

> [H]e went and preached to the spirits in prison.
>
> —1 Peter 3:19

> [He] has gone into heaven and is at the right hand of God, with angels, authorities, and powers subject to him.
>
> —1 Peter 3:22

> [T]hey will give account to him who is ready to judge the living and the dead.
>
> —1 Peter 4:5

> There is one body and one Spirit . . . one Lord,
> one faith, one baptism, one God and Father of us
> all.
>
> — Ephesians 4:4–6

There is a confessional quality to each of these statements, though they appear in many different contexts in various biblical books by several authors. That the Christian confession was an oath is clear from Philippians 2:9–11.

> Therefore God has highly exalted him and bestowed on him the name which is above every name, that at the name of Jesus every knee should bow, in heaven and on earth and under the earth, and every tongue confess that Jesus Christ is Lord, to the glory of God the Father.

The passage presents itself as a confession ("every tongue confess") and invokes the oracle in Isaiah in which God swears an oath by his own name: "By myself I have sworn . . . a word that shall not return: 'To me every knee shall bow, every tongue shall swear'" (Is 45:23).

The confessions of the New Covenant maintain the Old Covenant's insistent monotheism. Yet they also assert the Christian difference: that God's Son, Jesus, is also divine—he is Lord—and that there is one Spirit. Thus, already, the Church confessed a plurality of divine persons as one God. The creeds would bring together the doctrinal elements of this mystery in ways that were far more complete and clear.

◆ ◆ ◆

Already in the first generation of the Church, doctrinal unity is of paramount importance. Still, the Gospel is not reducible to doctrine. The Good News is a narrative; and the Apostles take care to tell the story whenever they preach (see, for example, Acts 2, 3, 10, and 13).

They tell the story in its barest outline: Jesus Christ died, was buried, rose again, and is exalted in glory. It is a curious fact that the Apostles, for the most part, skip over Jesus' moral instruction and miracles and fast-forward to the events of the last weeks of his earthly ministry. They proclaim his scandalous death, but seem to ignore his demonstrations of power: the feeding of multitudes, healing of lepers, and walking on water.

We will examine this pattern more closely later in the book. For now it is enough for us to observe that the essential details of Jesus' life—in the apostolic preaching and in the creedal confessions—are the stations of his Passion and Paschal Mystery. This pattern, fixed in the apostolic era, continues in every generation afterward and is enshrined in the classic creeds.

◆ ◆ ◆

In the New Testament, the confessions were signs of conversion and illumination. Peter received the doctrine of the Christ as an unmediated grace; in his confession, he actively accepted it and proclaimed it. Thomas, for his part, saw, believed, and professed his faith. It was the matter of a moment. Paul delivered what he had received, and he expected his congregation to confess it in turn, in the presence of many witnesses.

These are not merely instances of instruction. They are moments of conversion—the deep transformation of a human life. The confession is an outward sign of an interior change that is taking place.

Baptism was the ordinary place for such a declaration. Believers first received a summary of the Gospel—emphasizing the mysteries unseen and the doctrines that set Christians apart from everyone else. With their response they accepted the terms of the covenant, and with the sacrament they were received into the covenant family.

From that moment onward, they, as new Christians, would be *different*—different from what they had been and different from the rest of the world. They would be blessed to share divine life, now and forever. They would also be outcast, subject to persecution, and guilty—in the eyes of earthly courts—of a capital crime.

To confess the faith of Christians was a matter of enormous consequences. To confess faith in Jesus was to accept the stigma he bore—and to agree to share his inglorious death—in hope of a share in his glorious Resurrection.

Every confession was a pledge, too, to live by Jesus' truly revolutionary doctrine—the doctrine that made Christians different, drawing the fascination and fear of their neighbors.

With the *homologia*, Christians accepted the obligation of *martyria*—the Greek word for witness and the root of our English word "martyrdom." Often, in the generation of the Apostles, that witness demanded the shedding of blood. Always it demands a total gift of self.

CHAPTER 4

THE THUNDERING KANON

THE EARLY CHURCH POSSESSED LITTLE in the way of books. Christians, like everyone else, had no means to mass produce texts. The invention of the printing press was more than a thousand years off in the future. Literacy was a luxury enjoyed by a minority of the people of the world. And the Apostles themselves—the eventual authors of the sacred texts—began their ministry without recourse to any canonical Christian documents.

Yet the Gospel spread with astonishing speed—and it spread without pamphlets or leaflets, without catechisms or missals, without family Bibles or pocket-sized New Testaments. By the end of the first century, the Apostles had taken the faith to the limits of the known world.

The Apostles could not airdrop Bibles into the cities they evangelized. What they did was preach the Gospel. They presented the story of salvation in a summary way, with narrative and doctrinal elements. St. Peter's primordial sermon, on the day of the first Christian Pentecost, accomplishes this. He speaks of Jesus' death, Resurrection, Ascension into glory, and sending of the Spirit (Acts 2:22–33). He affirms Jesus' identity as Messiah and Lord.

Such compact summaries became a standard element in the preaching of the Apostles and in post-apostolic age. The early Fathers described these with the Greek word *kanon*, meaning "measure" or "rule." St. Paul had used the term similarly when he said: "Peace and mercy be upon all who walk by this rule, upon the Israel of God" (Gal 6:16).

The rule became a "measuring stick" of authentic Christianity, a yardstick of orthodoxy. The Fathers commonly used the word along with some other term denoting the ultimate standard for measurement. Thus, it appears most often as *kanon res aletheias*—"rule of truth"—but also as "rule of faith" and "rule of the Church." In the Latin-speaking Western Church, the term most commonly used was *regula fidei*, "rule of faith."

The faith of the Church was something preached, something given. When St. Paul laid down oral confession as a condition of salvation, he added: "But how are men . . . to believe in him of whom they have never heard? And how are they to hear without a preacher?" (Rom 10:14). The "rule" that was preached had to be heard and assimilated before it could be declared publicly—before individuals could make "the good confession in the presence of many witnesses" (1 Tim 6:12).

The rule of faith, then, is the general category we use to describe these primitive declarations of faith. Usually delivered in sermons and recited or accepted upon Baptism, they were summary statements of the most important—the most basic and essential—points of Christian faith.

◆ ◆ ◆

In the beginning they were simple. The primitive baptismal formula—the simple Trinitarian blessing—may have been an elementary rule of faith: "In the name of the Father and of the Son and of the Holy Spirit" (Mt 28:19). As we find it in the Gospel, it presents Trinitarian doctrine in a baptismal context. Jesus commanded the Apostles to "Go and baptize" all people in this way.

To the Galatians, St. Paul presented an implicitly Trinitarian faith along with a compressed narrative of Jesus' saving mission:

> But when the fullness of time had come, God sent his Son, born of a woman, born under the law, in order to redeem those who were under the law, so that we might receive adoption as children. And because you are children, God has sent the Spirit of his Son into our hearts, crying, "Abba! Father!" So you are no longer a slave but a child, and if a child then also an heir, through God.
>
> —Galatians 4:4–7

The First Letter of St. John, similarly, presents the story in outline form, with the expectation of a doctrinal confession in response. John's message, again like Paul's, is fundamentally Trinitarian, speaking of the respective roles and attributes of Father, Son, and Holy Spirit.

> By this you know the Spirit of God: every spirit which confesses that Jesus Christ has come in the flesh is of God. . . . In this the love of God was made manifest among us, that God . . . loved us and sent his Son to be the expiation for our sins. . . . By this we know that we abide in him and he in us, because he has given us of his own Spirit. And we have seen and testify that the Father has sent his Son as the Savior of the world. Whoever confesses that Jesus is the Son of God, God abides in him, and he in God.
>
> — 1 John 4:2, 9–10, 13–15

The essential apostolic preaching, then, presented a "rule" that was Trinitarian and historical in its content. It spoke of God's nature and his work in history; both were considered to be objects of faith. Both must be confessed by Christians at Baptism.

◆ ◆ ◆

It is clear from the letters of St. John that the Church of the first generation faced not only persecution from without, but also dissension from within. John preaches Jesus "come in the flesh," and in this he opposes the nascent heresy of the docetists—those who held that Jesus only *seemed* to be human and that his flesh was an illusion. "For many deceivers have gone out into the world, men who will not acknowledge the coming of Jesus Christ in the flesh; such a one is the deceiver and the antichrist" (2 Jn 1:7).

Such deceivers were numerous ("many"), and their false teaching had to be measured against a reliable rule of faith. And the docetists were not alone in their dissent. Already in the first generation there were the first eruptions of other heresies, and still others followed in the centuries afterward.

By the middle of the first century, the heresies were metastasizing through every land. St. Irenaeus of Lyon composed his multivolume work, *Against Heresies*, to counteract their spread. His intention was to measure each heretic's doctrine against the Church's rule and to train ordinary believers how to apply the same measure.

> He who retains unchangeable in his heart the rule of the truth which he received by means of baptism, will doubtless recognize the names, the expressions, and the parables taken from the Scriptures, but will by no means acknowledge the blasphemous use which these men make of them.[1]

---

[1] St. Irenaeus of Lyon, *Against the Heresies* 1.9.4.

Irenaeus was most concerned with heretics who denied the goodness of creation, some of whom even attributed the creation of the world to demons. Against them he insisted on certain elements of the ancient rule that identify the Creator with the God and Lord of the Old Testament and, furthermore, with the Father of Jesus Christ.

> The rule of truth that we hold is that there is one God Almighty, who made all things by his Word, and fashioned and formed, out of that which had no existence, all things that exist. So says the Scripture, to that effect: "By the word of the LORD the heavens were made, and all their host by the Spirit of his mouth" (Psalm 33:6). And again: "all things were made through him, and without him was not anything made that was made" (John 1:3). There is no exception or deduction stated; but the Father made all things by him, whether visible or invisible. . . . He who fashioned man is the God of Abraham, and the God of Isaac, and the God of Jacob, above whom there is no other God, nor initial principle, nor power, nor fullness. He is the Father of our Lord Jesus Christ, as we shall prove. Holding, therefore, this rule, we shall easily show . . . that these men have deviated from the truth.[2]

---

[2] Ibid., 1.22.1.

The rule, for Irenaeus, is the measure by which doctrine is tested and heretics are exposed. "This then is the order of the rule of our faith, and the foundation of the building, and the stability of our conversation."[3]

◆ ◆ ◆

The life of Irenaeus overlapped with that of Tertullian, a convert to the faith who wrote from Carthage in North Africa—and the two men showed similar concerns. Both wrote volumes of anti-heretical works. And both made explicit appeals to the rule of faith. Tertullian felt constrained to spell out the rule in explicit terms, and his terms sound increasingly like those that eventually found their way into the creeds.

We find his most concise statement of the rule in his treatise *On the Veiling of Virgins*. Like Irenaeus, he speaks of the rule as something distinct from any attempts to express it verbally—just as the Gospel is distinct from (though not separate from) the written gospels.

> The rule of faith, indeed, is altogether one, alone immovable and irreformable; the rule, to wit, of believing in one only God omnipotent, the Creator of the universe, and his Son Jesus Christ, born of the Virgin Mary, crucified under Pontius Pilate, raised again the third day from the dead, received in the heavens, sitting now at the right hand of the

---

[3]   St. Irenaeus of Lyon, *Demonstration of the Apostolic Preaching* 5.

Father, destined to come to judge living and dead through the resurrection of the flesh.[4]

The rule of faith is not the whole of the faith. It represents, rather, the most fundamental and essential teachings in the hierarchy of the truths of faith (see CCC 234).

And its expression, while generally accepted, was never codified in antiquity. It appears in similar but not identical verbal form in the works of authors as diverse and geographically dispersed as Irenaeus of Lyon, Tertullian of Carthage, Clement of Alexandria, Hippolytus of Rome, and many others.

Usually its expression was tailored to the demands of circumstance. If an author was battling a particular sort of heresy, he emphasized the doctrine that was challenged by the heretics. Thus Irenaeus expanded upon the goodness of creation, Tertullian on the triune Godhead, and Clement of Alexandria on the necessity of the Church.

Tertullian acknowledged that there is development in Christian doctrine as the Church gradually deepens its understanding of the truth. But all legitimate development is dependent upon the rule of faith and must never contradict it. "This law of faith being constant," he said, "the other succeeding points of discipline and conversation admit the 'novelty' of correction; the grace of God, to wit, operating and advancing even to the end." The rule

---

[4] Tertullian, *On the Veiling of Virgins* 1. See also his formulations in *Prescription Against Heretics* 13 and *Against Praxeas* 2.

is a safeguard against the excesses of theological speculation: "This rule, as it will be proved, was taught by Christ, and raises among ourselves no other questions than those which heresies introduce, and which make men heretics."[5]

◆ ◆ ◆

As the faith endured challenges and dissension—from persecutors and from heretics—the churches found it necessary to spell out the rule of faith in greater detail and with greater precision. In third-century Egypt, Origen prescribed seven general categories as essential to the rule: (1) the unity of God and his role as Creator; (2) the divinity of the Word, who was made flesh in Jesus Christ; (3) the worship of the Holy Spirit; (4) the immortality of the soul and the reality of judgment; (5) the existence of the devil and his angels; (6) the fact of creation in time; and (7) the divine authorship of the Scriptures.[6]

No one seems to have followed Origen's "rules for the rule"—not even Origen himself, whose various quasi-creedal summaries vary in their content.

But, through those first generations of the Church's life, we can see a movement toward standardization, or at least a strong desire for an established standard. The Fathers formulated different expressions—with different nuances, different emphases—for differing historical circumstances. Yet two centuries were certainly time enough

---

[5] Tertullian, *Prescription Against Heretics* 13.

[6] Origen, *On First Principles*, Preface 3–8.

to notice recurring patterns of provocation and response.

"Jesus Christ is the same yesterday and today and for ever" (Heb 13:8), so the target of true devotion remained always, in the words of Tertullian, immovable and irreformable. Still, at the dawn of the Christian era, St. Paul could exclaim: "O the depth of the riches and wisdom and knowledge of God! How unsearchable are his judgments and how inscrutable his ways!" (Rom 11:33). That statement was no less true in the third century.

In the Church's invocation of the rule of faith, we find pure reflections of both the mystery of God and the wonder of his people. No formula could contain a God infinite and eternal. It was God's very mystery that Christians sought to protect as they sought greater exactness in their confession of faith. It was a matter not simply of logic, but of love—a love divine and boundless, which the heretics of the fourth century would have bound up in time.

It was a matter of the family bond. The Rule of Faith conveyed the truth of the covenant—its story and its doctrine in barest outline.

CHAPTER 5

FROM FREEDOM TO FORMULA

AN ANCIENT TRADITION ASCRIBES the creation of the earliest creed to the Apostles themselves. St. Ambrose, in the year 389, speaks of such a creed, placing its authority alongside the authority of Scripture as he issues a warning for the heretics of his time:

> But if they will not believe the doctrines of the clergy, let them believe the oracles of Christ; let them believe the admonitions of Angels who say, "For with God nothing will be impossible" (Luke 1:37). Let them give credit to the Creed of the Apostles, which the Roman Church has always kept and preserved undefiled.[1]

By the last decade of the fourth century, the Roman creed was already so well established that a bishop as astute as Ambrose could assume it had "always" been there, and always reverently protected.

---

[1] St. Ambrose of Milan, *Letters* 42.5, from the Council of Milan to Pope Siricius.

Ambrose's contemporary, Rufinus of Aquileia, wrote a commentary on the Roman creed. He assumed that the ancient formula contained "the words of the Apostles in their native simplicity,"[2] and he preserved for all ages the legend of its composition.

> Our forefathers have handed down to us this tradition: After the Lord's ascension, at the coming of the Holy Spirit, tongues of flame settled upon each of the Apostles, so that they might speak diverse languages—so that no race however foreign, no tongue however barbarous, might be inaccessible to them and beyond their reach. . . . On the eve of departing from one another, they first mutually agreed upon a standard for their future preaching, lest, when separated, they might vary in any statements they should make to those whom they invite to believe in Christ. Gathered together, then, and filled with the Holy Spirit, they composed this brief formula of their future preaching, each contributing his individual sentence to one common summary: and they ordained that the rule thus framed should be given to those who believe.[3]

---

[2] Rufinus of Aquileia, *Commentary on the Apostles' Creed* 1.

[3] Ibid., 2.

Rufinus places this orderly gathering of the Apostles in stark contrast with a well-known passage from the Old Testament: the chaos brought about by the actions of the citizens of Babel. The men of Babel "built a tower of pride" and were "condemned to the confusion of tongues, so that no one might understand his neighbor's speech." The Apostles, on the other hand, "were building a tower of faith, and were endowed with the knowledge and understanding of all languages; so that the one might prove a sign and token of sin, the other of faith."

Rufinus presented the creed as a sign or symbol of the unity of the Christians, who everywhere and in every age professed the same faith. The antiquity of the creed was, for him, proof positive, as was its reputed origin with the Apostles, who were the Church's universal teachers.

Sign and symbol (Latin *signum* and Greek *symbolon*) were, in fact, the terms Rufinus used to describe the creed. He compared it to the standards that soldiers bear in battle: these indicate the army to which the soldiers belong. Christians who place themselves under the Apostles' Creed are declaring themselves to be on the side of the Apostles.

◆ ◆ ◆

It would be rash, perhaps, to dismiss these accounts out of hand. Both Ambrose and Rufinus were reputable and responsible scholars. But reputable and responsible scholars can be wrong. And the truth is that we possess no evidence to corroborate their story about the origins of the creed. In fact, the evidence we have seems to testify against their account.

If the Apostles had indeed produced a standard text for confession, it would likely appear somewhere in the documentary record of the first three centuries. But it does not. There would probably be some allusion, some passing reference to such a creed or its backstory. But there is none.

Still, there is strong evidence, very early in history, for the use of a standard baptismal creed in the Roman Church. Around 215, a Roman priest named Hippolytus compiled a book of liturgical texts that we know today as *The Apostolic Tradition*. He was a man of very conservative temperament, fighting what he perceived to be the lax and liberal tendencies of the popes of his time. His intention, he said in the opening lines of his book, was to preserve "the essence of the tradition that is proper for the churches. This is so that those who are well informed may keep the tradition that has lasted until now"—and that they may protect that deposit "against the fall or error which has recently occurred because of ignorance and ignorant people."[4]

Hippolytus had a deep desire—and a practical need—to demonstrate the ancient pedigree for the practices he advocated in his book. So it is likely that he would claim

---

[4] St. Hippolytus of Rome, *The Apostolic Tradition* 1.2–4.

for antiquity only what could plausibly be put forward as ancient in 215. The practices he described probably reach back at least to the middle of the second century, if not further.

A universal creed written by the Apostles would certainly have appealed to Hippolytus, but he makes no mention of it. What he does provide is the first recorded instance of a fixed creed. It appears in his account of the baptismal liturgy and it is presented as a series of questions and answers.

> When each of those to be baptized has gone down into the water, the one baptizing shall lay hands on each of them, asking, "Do you believe in God the Father Almighty?" And the one being baptized shall answer, "I believe." He shall then baptize each of them once, laying his hand upon each of their heads.

> Then he shall ask, "Do you believe in Jesus Christ, the Son of God, who was born of the Holy Spirit and the Virgin Mary, who was crucified under Pontius Pilate, and died, and rose on the third day living from the dead, and ascended into heaven, and sat down at the right hand of the Father, the one coming to judge the living and the dead?" When each has answered, "I believe," he shall baptize a second time.

Then he shall ask, "Do you believe in the Holy Spirit and the Holy Church and the resurrection of the flesh?" Then each being baptized shall answer, "I believe." And thus let him baptize the third time.[5]

The question-and-answer format would become a standard method of confessing the faith. Remember that most people in the average congregation would have had little or no ability to read; and, in any event, mass-produced texts did not exist. Recitation depended on rote memory—or the kind of call and response we find in the creed of *The Apostolic Tradition*.

The interrogatory form was proper to Baptism for another, perhaps more important reason. It confirmed the sense of the rite as a *sacramentum*—a term familiar to Romans from secular culture and especially military usage. A *sacramentum* was a solemn oath that was legally binding. Tertullian had already applied the term to the Christian rites of initiation. The New Testament scholar Edward Gordon Selwyn notes that the interrogatory form arose naturally because the first Christians believed "baptism was a seal of contract given by a good conscience towards God." As such it was a juridical act, to which a "test-question" or "solemn interrogatories" might be applied.[6] The creeds, then, *strengthened* the sense that Baptism marked a covenant.

---

[5] Ibid., 21.12–18.
[6] Edward Gordon Selwyn, *The First Epistle of St. Peter* (New York: MacMillan, 1947), 205–206.

The interrogatory creed in Hippolytus is similar to the presentations of the rule of faith we find in Tertullian and Irenaeus. Some lines recur rather exactly. All, of course, depend upon the same New Testament passages (which we cited in Chapter 3) and echo their language.

◆ ◆ ◆

Through the second and third centuries we see a certain movement toward standardization—not only of the Christian confessions, but of other areas of the Church's life. It is a movement, as the theologian Allan Bouley has described it, "from freedom to formula."[7]

As the Church grew and spread to lands distant from its origins, Christians desired to preserve the faith intact even as they adapted its expression to different languages and cultures. The pattern—from freedom to formula—is evident even in the first generation. When "the disciples were increasing in number" (Acts 6:1), the Apostles found it necessary to assign specific duties to different clerical offices (Acts 6:2–4). By the turn of the century, their division of labor—the three-tiered hierarchy of bishop, presbyter, and deacon—would be fairly standard in the Church, as witnessed by the letters of Ignatius of Antioch in 107.[8]

---

[7] Allan Bouley, OSB, *From Freedom to Formula: The Evolution of the Eucharistic Prayer from Oral Improvisation to Written Texts* (Washington, DC: Catholic University of America, 1981).

[8] See St. Ignatius of Antioch, *Letter to the Magnesians* 2, 6, 13; *Trallians* 2; *Philadelphians* 7.

The liturgy underwent a similar pattern of development. In the *Didache*, a document of the first century, we find texts of prayers to be used in the Eucharist, but they end with a rubric that seems to allow extemporaneous additions as well: "But allow the prophets to hold Eucharist as they will."[9] By the time of Hippolytus we find the Church still providing fixed texts, but permitting some improvisation.

> The bishop shall give thanks according to all that was said above. It is not at all necessary that he prays with the very same words given above, as though by an effort of memory giving thanks to God. Each shall pray whatever is according to his ability. If someone has the ability to pray a lengthy and solemn prayer, that is well. If someone else, in praying, offers a short prayer, this is not to be prevented. That prayer must only be correct in orthodoxy.[10]

At the beginning of the third century we see an increasing concern for orthodoxy in prayer and practice. This is understandable, as the Church was roiled already by a variety of heresies, many of which were present in Rome and exercised some influence (and temptation) among Christians there. It became increasingly import-

---

[9] *Didache* 10.7.
[10] St. Hippolytus of Rome, *The Apostolic Tradition* 9.3–5.

ant to get the prayers right—"correct in orthodoxy."

Against these challenges, the Church began the process of standardizing its offices, rites, scriptural canon, disciplines, and its rule of faith. In the question-and-answer creed of Hippolytus we can practically watch the development taking place.

◆ ◆ ◆

In 1982 the theologian Joseph Ratzinger (later Pope Benedict XVI) published his magisterial *Principles of Catholic Theology*. In it he considers the authority of the Fathers "in the synthesis of faith."[11] He notes that it is from the time of the Fathers—roughly the first millennium—that we have received several "historical concretizations,"[12] among them the Church's great liturgical families, the canon of the New Testament, and the fixity of the classic creeds.

Why do we recognize such authority in the work of men such as Hippolytus and Ambrose? After all, as Ratzinger notes, Jesus himself represents the fullness of God's self-revelation.

But revelation, he explains, is a form of communication, and as such it assumes the existence of two parties in an exchange. It assumes a word and a response.

The time of the Fathers was the Church's active response to God's revelation in Jesus Christ. The work of

---

[11] Joseph Cardinal Ratzinger, *Principles of Catholic Theology: Building Stones for a Fundamental Theology* (San Francisco: Ignatius Press, 1987), 147.

[12] Ibid., 148.

the Fathers was the Church's great "Amen" to the gift of salvation. We see their "Amen" in the forms they developed for the rule of faith, the Mass, the Bible, and the Church itself.

The creed of Hippolytus, then—the ancient creed of the Church of Rome—gives us something more than a testimony. It is a vivid image, in its questions and answers, of the Church's eager, active response to God's Word.

First comes the question: "Do you believe . . . ?"

And, from the second century onward, the Church answers with an ever more unanimous voice: "I believe!"

CHAPTER 6

THE CROWN OF THE COUNCIL

THE EMPEROR CONSTANTIUS, son of Constantine, had contempt for Pope Liberius, and the contempt fairly drips from the transcript of his interrogation.

Liberius was summoned before the throne because he had stood with Athanasius, the patriarch of Alexandria in Egypt, in upholding the true divinity of Christ as it was defined at the Council of Nicaea and expressed in that council's creed. Though an overwhelming majority of the bishops at Nicaea had approved the language of the creed, the next generation was not so enthusiastic. In fact, it had largely backslidden to the heresy of Arius, whose false teaching had occasioned the council.

Despite the Church's overwhelming condemnation, the heresy continued to spread—so rapidly that St. Jerome described it accurately and memorably: It was as if "the world had suddenly woke up to find itself Arian."[1]

Now, in 355, just thirty years after the Council, the emperor himself was a committed Arian. Because of the

---

[1] St. Jerome, *Dialogue Against the Luciferians* 19.

emperor's influence, many Arians had been elevated to the office of bishop throughout the world.

Constantius was furious that his efforts to Arianize the Church were encountering roadblocks—in two substantial men, presiding over two extremely important and influential churches.

"Who are *you*—," Constantius asked the pope. "Who are *you* to stand up for Athanasius against the world?"[2]

Three times in the interrogation the emperor uses the phrase "the whole world" to describe the extent of current opposition to the faith of Nicaea—and specifically Athanasius. "The whole world has condemned him."

Such sweeping statements stuck, and even today historians describe the situation as *Athanasius contra mundum*—"Athanasius against the world."

Indeed, both Athanasius and Liberius would spend years in harsh exile for defending the faith enshrined in the Nicene Creed. But what exactly was the faith that made them stand up to the world?

◆ ◆ ◆

The crisis that led to the Council of Nicaea—the crisis that provoked a creed—began in the year 318. Alexander, then the Patriarch of Alexandria, was discussing the doctrine of the Trinity with a group of his priests. One of them, Arius, stood up to challenge Alexander and accuse

---

[2] Theodoret, *Church History* 2.13.

his bishop of heresy. At that meeting and afterward, Arius created a stir in the city. As he articulated his case against Alexander, it became clear that Arius considered Christ, the Son of God, to be subordinate to the Father—to be a creature, though the greatest of creatures. Jesus was "god," according to Arius, but only because God adopted him and gave him the gift of divinity. For Arius, Jesus could be considered "god" only if we put the word in quotation marks. For Arius, only the Father was eternal. The Son of God was neither coeternal nor coequal to the Father. There was a time, said Arius, when the Son did not exist. Arius coined a slogan, "There was when he was not," which he wove into hymns with catchy tunes, easily remembered.

Alexander thought it best to convene a local synod to consider the matter. That assembly weighed both sides and judged Arius's doctrine to be heretical. The priest was condemned and exiled.

But exile only made matters worse. Arius found new audiences—and bishops and lay people who were sympathetic to his teaching. It spread like a virus, mutating as it spread. The emperor at the time was Constantine, who had only recently legalized the practice of the Christian faith after centuries of Roman persecution. He worried that the fragile "Peace of the Church" was already falling apart as, from church to church, each Christian faction condemned all others. In 325 he sent a representative to summon a council in Syrian Antioch. The council published a creed, which was to be a test and measure of true doctrine.

But prominent churchmen challenged the findings of that council, and so Constantine called the bishops of the world to meet in Nicaea, a suburb of the imperial capital—where the emperor himself could monitor the proceedings.

It did not go well for Arius. Alexander's spokesman at the Council of Nicaea was a brilliant young deacon named Athanasius, a man fiercely devoted to the tradition. The assembled bishops decided overwhelmingly in favor of Alexander and against Arius.

Augmenting the declarations that were already established—the Roman baptismal creed and the creed of the earlier synod at Antioch—the bishops promulgated a new and fuller rule, which became known as the Nicene Creed.

> We believe in one God, the Father Almighty, maker of all things visible and invisible. And in one Lord Jesus Christ, the Son of God, the only-begotten, begotten of the Father; that is, from the substance of the Father, God from God, Light from Light, true God from true God, begotten, not made, consubstantial with the Father. Through him all things were made, both in heaven and on earth. For us men and for our salvation he came down and was incarnate and was made man. He

suffered, and the third day he rose again; he ascended into heaven. From thence he shall come to judge the living and the dead. And in the Holy Spirit.

The creed was published at the head of the decrees of the council, and it was delivered throughout the world. Alexander of Alexandria died just a few months after the council, after naming Athanasius as his successor as patriarch.

Alexander could rest in peace. But Athanasius would hardly know rest through all his years as patriarch. Arius had powerful allies who continued to spread his errors. The conclusions of the Council of Nicaea—and its creed—were challenged at every turn. Athanasius was exiled repeatedly. Matters got much worse in 337, when the emperor Constantine died and was succeeded by his three sons, of whom only one would reign for very long.

That sole surviving monarch was Constantius II, the interrogator of Pope Liberius, whom we met at the beginning of this chapter. And Constantius was determined to see Arianism prevail.

◆ ◆ ◆

Arius based his arguments on a selective reading of Scripture, reading these passages apart from their context, apart from the other Scriptures—and, most especially, apart from the Church's worship.

Athanasius accused Arius of arrogating to himself an authority that belonged only to the Church—which alone was entrusted with the apostolic tradition summarized in the rule of faith. Arius' interpretation of Scripture was idiosyncratic and opposed to the long-established confessions and worship of the Church.

Athanasius charged that the ancient Rite of Baptism was nonsensical if interpreted according to the doctrine of Arius. The Trinitarian confession of the rule of faith and the threefold immersion of Baptism both bespeak an *equal* divinity of Father, Son, and Holy Spirit. Nowhere in the rule of faith do we find any suggestion of gradations of divinity. Nowhere do the early Christian declarations—from Irenaeus, Tertullian, Origen, and others—suggest a difference-in-kind between any divine person and the others.

Arius, on the other hand, was uneasy with terms like "Father" and "Son," because he believed them to describe conditions that were bound by time. If there was a time when the Son "was not," then there was a time when God was not truly "Father." Thus, Arius gravitated to other titles for Jesus' pre-incarnational existence, such as Word.

Athanasius argued from Scripture, but he argued most insistently from the practice and prayer of the Church. The heresy of Arius could not possibly be reconciled with the Rite of Baptism as it had been practiced since the time of the Apostles. Arianism foundered on Matthew 28:19:

"Go therefore and make disciples of all nations, baptizing them in the name of the Father and of the Son and of the Holy Spirit."[3] "The Arians," Athanasius complained, "do not baptize into Father and Son, but into Creator and creature, and into Maker and work."[4]

Athanasius' principle of interpretation, practiced by all the Fathers, was summarized in the following century as "*Lex orandi lex credendi*"—"The law of praying is the law of believing." Athanasius knew Jesus to be God because the Church had always identified Jesus, along with the Father and Holy Spirit, as an object of worship. Athanasius knew Jesus to be God also because the baptismal formula depended upon the coeternal deity of the Son. The liturgy—for Athanasius, Liberius, and all the Church Fathers—was a medium of tradition.

Indeed it seems that the primary use of the rule of faith was in the baptismal rite—as a test and declaration of orthodoxy. Whether as a recited creed or a series of questions, the public confession of the rule of faith proved that the catechumen was ready and willing to enter into covenant with God. The baptismal covenant was creedal from the generation of the Apostles, and the confession was consistently Trinitarian, as far back as the Church could remember.

If Athanasius and Liberius were willing to set themselves against "the whole world," it's because the whole

---

[3] See Athanasius, *Discourses Against the Arians* 4.21.
[4] Ibid., 2.42. See also sections 1.9.34; 2.41; and 4.25 in the same work.

world had set itself against the apostolic faith, the tradition, the rule, expressed in the Creed of Nicaea.

◆ ◆ ◆

The creed produced by the council was, for the most part, made up of creedal statements that had been in use for generations before the council. The great exception to that rule is the word we translate as "consubstantial." This word (in Greek, *homoousios*) was added specifically to counteract the poisonous doctrine of Arius. It describes the close and inseparable union between the Son and the Father. They are, literally, "of the same substance."

Some of the council Fathers raised objections to the use of the word *homoousios*. It drew from Greek philosophy and could be found nowhere in Scripture. It had no Hebrew equivalent in the Old Testament. And none of the earlier Christians had used it in their preaching or speculative theology. Should Christians use words from outside the tradition to explain and defend the terms of the tradition?

In retrospect their objections can seem easy to dismiss. *Homoousios* has been "traditional" for us for 1,700 years. Its use, again for us, goes back almost to the beginning. Nicene faith is, for many mainstream Christians, synonymous with Christian faith. It seems to us that this is the way things have always been done.

But the Fathers of Nicaea were already looking back on almost three hundred years of Christian practice, and three centuries is a long time. Those men, moreover, had a horror of innovation, a dread fear of doing anything that would compromise the faith they had received intact from the Apostles—the fullness of God's self-revelation in the person of Jesus Christ.

When the council applied the vocabulary of Plato to the exposition of Scripture, they were doing so *for the sake of the Church's understanding of Scripture.* After acknowledging that "the Council of Nicaea clearly went beyond the language of Scripture in describing Jesus," Cardinal Joseph Ratzinger goes on to explain why this was necessary.

> What does "of one substance" really mean? The answer is this: the term is used solely as a translation of the word "Son" into philosophical language. And why is it necessary to translate it? Well, whenever faith begins to reflect, the question arises as to what, in reality, the word "Son" might mean as applied to Jesus.[5]

The Fathers adopted a technical philosophical term in order to safeguard the traditional reading of Scripture against the subversion of Arian innovation. Arius, drawing only from selected Scripture passages—wrenched

---

[5] Joseph Cardinal Ratzinger, "Seven Theses on Christology and the Hermeneutic of Faith," *Letter & Spirit* 3 (2007): 202.

from context—was succeeding in the deconstruction of the Church's ancient rule and rites.

After the council, as the "Homoousians" prevailed, the Arians sought another compromise. They proposed that the Church employ a slightly different term: *homoiousios*. The word differed in only one letter, an additional *iota*, a lower-case *i*. *Homoiousios* meant "of similar substance" rather than "of the same substance." And, many Christian leaders, weary of the argument, were willing to give in.

But Athanasius saw that "one *iota's* difference" threatened the entire edifice of Christian faith. He refused to accommodate the creed to the uses of heresy. And he suffered for his refusal.

◆ ◆ ◆

To a modern reader, however, it is immediately evident that the Creed of Nicaea (as rendered above) differs significantly from the Nicene Creed Catholics today recite at Mass. The text approved at Nicaea says almost nothing, for example, about the Holy Spirit—stopping abruptly after a bare mention.

The text we call the Nicene Creed was actually elaborated upon and approved in 381 at the First Council of Constantinople, shortly after the death of Athanasius. By then, the Church's worship of the Holy Spirit had begun to suffer the same challenges as the worship of Jesus had suffered in the previous generation. Athanasius responded to these as well, though the task of a full refutation fell to younger men, especially the Cappadocian Fathers: St. Basil the Great, St. Gregory of Nazianzus, and St. Gregory of Nyssa.

Gregory of Nazianzus presided at the Council of Constantinople and oversaw the drafting of the creed we use today. We call it Nicene, though, technically, it is Niceno-Constantinopolitan. (Thanks be to God for abbreviations.)

> I believe in one God,
> the Father almighty,
> maker of heaven and earth,
> of all things visible and invisible.
> I believe in one Lord Jesus Christ,
> the Only Begotten Son of God,
> born of the Father before all ages.
> God from God, Light from Light,
> true God from true God,
> begotten, not made, consubstantial with the Father;
> through him all things were made.
> For us men and for our salvation
> he came down from heaven,
> and by the Holy Spirit was incarnate of the
>   Virgin Mary,
> and became man.
> For our sake he was crucified under Pontius Pilate,
> he suffered death and was buried,

and rose again on the third day
in accordance with the Scriptures.
He ascended into heaven
and is seated at the right hand of the Father.
He will come again in glory
to judge the living and the dead
and his kingdom will have no end.
I believe in the Holy Spirit, the Lord, the giver of life,
who proceeds from the Father,
who with the Father and the Son is adored and
    glorified,
who has spoken through the prophets.
I believe in one, holy, catholic and apostolic Church.
I confess one Baptism for the forgiveness of sins
and I look forward to the resurrection of the dead
and the life of the world to come. Amen.

Careful readers will note one difference still between this ancient text and the creed we recite at Mass. But we'll take up that small difference, too, in a later chapter.

CHAPTER 7

THE SETTING OF THE CREED

"TRANSPARENCY" IS TODAY CONSIDERED a great virtue. In the Church we think it's best to keep no secrets. We sing "All Are Welcome" at our liturgies. The central mysteries of the faith are discussed familiarly in books (like this one) that are readily available in stores that sell greeting cards, breath mints, and popular music. Images of our sacraments are even emblazoned on T-shirts and bumper stickers.

It's difficult for us to imagine a time when this was not so. It's hard to re-enter a world where Christianity was new and ordinary citizens knew hardly anything about it. Elements of the faith could be easily misunderstood. The cross, for example, was the most grotesque form of public torture and execution, reserved for humiliation of slaves and those who were guilty of heinous crimes. Pagans could not fathom the early Christians' reverence for the cross.

Other marks of Christianity were badly misconstrued by pagan propagandists. The Eucharist was portrayed as cannibalism—a feast of human flesh and blood. Christian marriage was portrayed as incest because believers called one another "brother" and "sister." The doctrine of the Trinity was mocked as absurdity: three could not equal one.

Christians came to expect incomprehension, and so they protected the mysteries of faith with a reverent silence. Historians refer to this as the "discipline of secrecy" (*arcana disciplina*). Jesus himself had counseled his disciples: "To you it has been given to know the secrets of the kingdom of heaven, but to them it has not been given" (Mt 13:11). Thus: "Do not give dogs what is holy; and do not throw your pearls before swine, lest they trample them under foot and turn to attack you" (Mt 7:6). In his letter that dealt most extensively with the ritual life of the Church, St. Paul said: "But we impart a secret and hidden wisdom of God" (1 Cor 2:7).

The earliest creeds *seem* to keep no such reserve. They speak plainly about God's triune nature. The statements they make are plain, but the claims are bold: that there is one God; that the one God is a communion of three persons; that one of those persons was born of a virgin—and suffered; that the divine person truly died and then rose from the dead; that every human body, though decayed and destroyed, will rise again.

The creeds *seem* to protect no secrets. But it's important to know that the creeds *themselves* were secrets, and they were protected by the strictest discipline. And this was true not only in times of persecution, but even almost a century after the faith was legalized.

The proper setting for the creed, even then, was not in the marketplace or even in books. Its "publicity" was strictly limited. The creed's "public" was the Christian assembly. Its place was the liturgy.

◆ ◆ ◆

From the beginning, the Church's confessions—its rule of faith and its creeds—hovered near the liturgy. The New Testament references to confession (before witnesses) imply the presence of Christians assembled at a Baptism. Later accounts of the rule, such as we find in Tertullian, are more explicit about the baptismal setting for the use of the rule of faith.

It is likely, as we have shown, that the confessions became increasingly detailed as the Church faced new heresies. Against the docetists, it was necessary for a new Christian to state his or her belief that the Son of God was truly born, truly suffered, and truly died. Against the gnostics, it was necessary to declare one's allegiance to God as Creator of both heaven and earth and all things, visible and invisible. Against the Marcionites, it was necessary to profess that God had spoken through the prophets. Against the Arians, it was necessary to affirm that Jesus was true God from true God.

Through the Rite of Baptism people entered the covenant family. Through their confession of faith they confirmed that they accepted the terms of the covenant. They recognized that they were becoming truly Christian and nothing else. They would accept no substitutes for the faith of the Catholic Church.

The "handing on" (in Latin, *traditio*) of the creed was a specific rite in the process of initiation. It took place shortly before Baptism, and the delivery was entirely oral. St. Ambrose, in fact, specified most emphatically that the creed must *never* be committed to paper:

> I want you to be well aware of this: the creed must not be written down. . . . Why not? Because we have received it in a way that was not meant to be written. What then must you do? Remember it. . . . Go over the creed in your mind; I insist, in your mind. Why? So that you may not fall into the habit, by repeating it aloud to yourself, of starting to repeat it among the catechumens or the heretics.[1]

St. Augustine, writing decades later, issues the same command on several occasions.[2] The content of the creed was a mystery—a secret—that properly belonged only to initiated Christians.

The creed was "handed on," from bishop to catechumens, and then "handed back" (*redditio*) at (or near) the

---

[1] St. Ambrose of Milan, *Explanation of the Creed* 9.
[2] See, for example, *Sermons* 212.2 and 214.1 and *Of Faith and the Creed* 1.

time of Baptism. In some places the creed was recited from memory. In others it was conducted as a dialogue.

Augustine considered the creed to be a required part of the Rite of Baptism. He identified the creed with Baptism, which was its normal context. He even went so far as to call the creed itself a *sacramentum*,[3] though he surely did not mean the term in its later, technical sense[4] (meaning the seven central grace-bearing rites of the Church). The root meaning of *sacramentum* is "oath," and Augustine treats the creed as a symbol or sign of the binding covenant that is Baptism.

At this point in history, "creed" is still a somewhat fluid construct—though the Nicene Creed was already a century old and the creed of Constantinople was also well known. Augustine, nevertheless, uses three different creeds in his various catechetical works, and none appears to be a conciliar product! One is the creed he knew from his own training in Milan, another is a local African creed, and the third is of unknown provenance. They are similar in form and content, and they show that a certain commonality or catholicity was expected in a baptismal confession.

Only in the second half of the first millennium do we begin to see a standardization of use. By the year 1000 almost all churches were using the Apostles' Creed, the Nicene Creed, or both.

---

[3] See *Sermons* 228.3 and *Letters* 93.11.46.

[4] See Daniel G. Van Slyke, "The Changing Meanings of *Sacramentum*: Historical Sketches," *Antiphon* 11:3 (2007): 245–279.

◆ ◆ ◆

Today we most often encounter the creed when we attend Sunday Mass in a parish. Still in our time we see that the creed's natural habitat is the liturgy.

It seems, however, that the churches were at first hesitant to take the additional step of including the creed in the Church's covenant meal, the Eucharistic liturgy. Why? Quite likely because it was considered to be redundant. The ancient prayers of thanksgiving—the Eucharistic prayers—included capsule summaries of salvation history and brief narratives of the events of the life of Christ. Thus, the Eucharistic prayer itself had creedal content and was itself a kind of creed.

In the East, the Nicene Creed was read customarily only during the Good Friday liturgy. In the early sixth century the Patriarch of Constantinople required that it be recited at every Eucharistic liturgy. Writing around 630, St. Maximus the Confessor praised this most public use of the creed—"the profession by all"—for its catechetical and devotional value. In this way, by imposing the creed at every Eucharist, the Church regularly rehearsed the major milestones of salvation history, and so inspired the congregation to gratitude for the divine favors.[5]

Scholars today note that, as the congregational recitation of the creed became more common, the priests took to praying the Eucharistic prayers silently or *sotto voce.* "After the eclipse of the audible anaphora, the function of

---

[5] See St. Maximus the Confessor, *The Church's Mystagogy* 18.

guiding the thankful recollection of biblical events fell to other liturgical elements, especially the creed."[6]

Why was the common recitation of the creed established at that particular point in history? Because the Church, after two centuries of contentious Christological heresies—Arian, Semi-Arian, Nestorian, and Monophysite—wanted to unify its people and confirm their faith.

There can be no better place for this than the Eucharistic liturgy, which was designed to bring about the unity of the Church. "Because there is one bread, we who are many are one body, for we all partake of the one bread" (1 Cor 10:17).

Jesus established the Eucharist as "the new covenant" in his blood (Lk 22:20). So it is, like Baptism, a sign of the covenant. It is a renewal of the oath, the *sacramentum*, that binds the believer to Christ.

It is important, then, that the believer truly know Christ as he is revealed in the Gospels and confessed in the creeds.

And it is interesting to note that, with the introduction of the creed into the Mass, the period of the ancient Christological heresies came to a decisive end.

---

[6]   See Derek Krueger, *Liturgical Subjects: Christian Ritual, Biblical Narrative, and the Formation of the Self in Byzantium* (Philadelphia: University of Pennsylvania Press, 2014), 124.

CHAPTER 8

POINTS OF LIGHT

WHEN WE WANT TO UNDERSTAND something complex, we tend to break it down to its constituent parts and then find categories for its various components. There is nothing particularly modern or "scientific" about this. It's what Origen did when he wanted to present the Gospel in the third century. He said he discerned "certain points" that the Apostles "delivered with utmost clarity" because they were essential and "necessary to everyone, even to those who seemed somewhat dull in the investigation of divine knowledge."[1]

Origen considered the rule of faith as it was expounded in his day, and he believed it was best understood as divided into eight "particular points." They were, in brief:

1. That there is one God, and he is the Creator.
2. That Jesus Christ is the true Son of God.
3. That the Holy Spirit is associated in worship with the Father and Son.

---

[1]   Origen, *On First Principles*, Preface, 3.

4. That the soul will be judged and rewarded or punished.
5. That human beings possess free will.
6. That the devil and demons exist.
7. That the world was created and had a definite beginning in time.
8. That the Scriptures are divinely inspired.[2]

It is an unusual division and bears distinctive marks of its historical context. Origen shows special concern for the orthodox Christian doctrine of creation, because it was challenged in his time by certain philosophers (who believed that matter was uncreated and eternal) and by gnostic Christians (who believed that the material world was inherently evil, the work of a demon).

In Origen we find one way to divide up the Gospel for study: to consider it in light of current controversies.

But most of the ancients were concerned more to find the eternal and immutable. So they divided the portions of the rule—and later the creeds—according to different methods. They are all useful, and the rationale for each is illuminating.

The Fathers tended to divide the creed into two, three, or twelve segments. In this chapter I want to briefly consider each of these approaches in turn.

---

[2] Ibid., Preface 4–8.

◆ ◆ ◆

It's natural for us, first, to divide things in half. We look at humanity, for example, and draw sweeping conclusions: "There are two kinds of people in this world. . . ."

When some people look at the creed, they distinguish two kinds of statements in it. They divide the lines into statements about the *nature of God* and statements about the *works of God*—who God is and what he has done. Paragraph 236 of the Catechism of the Catholic Church gives us a helpful explanation of this approach, using the original Greek terms employed by the early Christians.

> The Fathers of the Church distinguish between theology (*theologia*) and economy (*oikonomia*). "Theology" refers to the mystery of God's inmost life within the Blessed Trinity and "economy" to all the works by which God reveals himself and communicates his life. Through the *oikonomia* the *theologia* is revealed to us; but conversely, the *theologia* illuminates the whole *oikonomia*. God's works reveal who he is in himself; the mystery of his inmost being enlightens our understanding of all his works. So it is, analogously, among human persons. A person discloses himself in his actions, and the better we know a person, the better we understand his actions.

From the creeds we gather much in the way of theology—much about God's nature: God is one, and there is only one God; God is Father; God is a Trinity of persons; God is eternal and uncreated; God the Son is coeternal with the Father; the Spirit of God is coequal with the Father and Son and "proceeds" from them.

We gather much also in the way of economy: God is the Creator of everything; the Father created the universe "through" the Son; the Son "became man" for the salvation of human beings; the Holy Spirit gives life and has spoken through the prophets; God continues his work of salvation through the Church and its sacraments; God will raise everyone from death for judgment and just reward.

From the creed, then, we learn that all creation is caught up in a drama that sweeps from the beginning of time to its end. There is a narrative arc to the history not only of humanity, but of the cosmos—"all things visible and visible." The cast of this drama includes everyone alive, everyone who ever lived, and everyone who will live. All will rise and be judged for the actions and omissions, small and great, of their everyday lives.

The Son of God "became man" and so chose, from all the natures he created, to share just one as his own. The creed tells us this. God assumed human nature and thus restored the dignity given to our race at creation, when Adam was made in God's image and likeness (Gen 1:26–27).

Theology and economy are mutually illuminating. The cosmos makes sense, ultimately, only when we contemplate it in light of the Creator. And the Creator himself is evident in the design of the cosmos. As St. Paul put it: "Ever since the creation of the world [God's] invisible nature, namely, his eternal power and deity, has been clearly perceived in the things that have been made" (Rom 1:20).

Apart from this narrative, it is difficult also to sustain the ideas that stand at the heart of our civilization: human dignity, for instance, and human equality. These notions depend upon the biblical account of creation, Incarnation, and redemption—the account that the Church rehearses whenever a congregation recites the creed.

This is the advantage of examining the creed in terms of theology and economy. We learn to review the story line of all the Scriptures—not just one book or another, but the whole narrative, in both testaments. We learn to do this whenever we recite the creed. And we come to find our place in the drama, which is still unfolding.

◆ ◆ ◆

If it is natural to divide a topic in two, it is surely *super*natural to divide the Christian confession in three. The grounds for such a division are purely divine.

Very early in Christian history we find St. Irenaeus insisting upon a threefold confession of the rule of faith. His organizing principle, of course, is the Blessed Trinity.

This then is the order of the rule of our faith, and the foundation of the building, and the stability of our conversation: God, the Father, not made, not material, invisible; one God, the creator of all things: this is the first point of our faith.

The second point is the Word of God, Son of God, Christ Jesus our Lord, who was manifested to the prophets according to the form of their prophesying and according to the method of the dispensation of the Father: through whom all things were made; who also at the end of the times, to complete and gather up all things, was made man among men, visible and tangible, in order to abolish death and show forth life and produce a community of union between God and man.

And the third point is the Holy Spirit, through whom the prophets prophesied, and the fathers learned the things of God, and the righteous were led forth into the way of righteousness; and who in the end of the times was poured out in a new way a upon mankind in all the earth, renewing man unto God.

And for this reason the baptism of our regeneration proceeds through these three points: God the

Father bestowing on us regeneration through his
Son by the Holy Spirit.[3]

Down through history, most meditations upon the
creed have followed this sequence, connecting the Trinitarian confession with the three immersions of Baptism.
There is nothing accidental about that connection.

Through the dogma of the Trinity, we learn that God
is a communion of persons. We learn that God is love and
bears a familial name denoting fatherhood and sonship.
God himself is a communion, a family, a plurality in loving unity.

Through the Gospel we discover that we, too, are—by
means of Baptism—given membership in that covenant
family. Again, it is no accident that the first proto-creed
was both Trinitarian and baptismal, and revealed by Jesus
himself (Mt 28:19). As the great scholar Cardinal Jean
Daniélou noted:

We should not forget the fact that "the Covenant"
was one of our Lord's names in primitive Christianity. . . . Baptism is our introduction into this
covenant.[4]

Even today, "Covenant" remains one of the Lord's
names, by virtue of the Trinitarian confession of the

---

[3] St. Irenaeus of Lyon, *Demonstration of the Apostolic Preaching* 5.
[4] Jean Daniélou, S.J., "The Sacraments and the History of Salvation," in *The Liturgy and the Word of God* (Collegeville: Liturgical Press, 1959).

creed; and so the threefold consideration of the creed has been fairly standard since Irenaeus. It will certainly inform the remainder of our chapters in this book.

◆ ◆ ◆

As we move from three to twelve divisions, we move from the most sublime to the most colorful, picturesque, and archetypal.

In Chapter 5 we encountered the "creation story" of the old Roman Creed as it was told by Rufinus of Aquilieia and St. Ambrose. That story divides the ancient creed into twelve articles and claims that they were given as oracles, one by one, to the Apostles gathered on Pentecost Sunday. In later elaborations, each article was assigned to a specific Apostle. Thus, St. Peter stepped forward and said: "I believe in God the Father Almighty." His brother St. Andrew followed, saying: "And in Jesus Christ, his only Son." And so it went until the last Apostle called by God, St. Matthias, who replaced Judas, came forward and professed his belief in "life everlasting."

The twentieth-century scholar Cardinal Henri de Lubac said that this story probably represented "a preacher's ingenious trick to make a catechism lesson more stimulating."[5] While he downplays the historicity of the account, he notes its profound Christian, and specifically biblical, resonances. These are noted by no less a saint

---

[5] Henri de Lubac, *The Christian Faith: An Essay on the Structure of the Apostles' Creed* (San Francisco: Ignatius Press, 1986) 35.

than Bonaventure, the twelfth-century Doctor of the Church. The event "had been prefigured," Bonaventure said,

> in the past by the Holy Spirit in the Book of Joshua, under the form of the twelve men who, chosen by the one whose very name was a figure of Jesus Christ, took twelve stones from the bed of the Jordan to build the altar of the Lord.[6]

Here we see the product of an imagination formed by Christian piety and the Bible's own methods of interpretation. Twelve men take twelve stones from the river associated with Baptism—the Jordan—and they use these stones to build a holy altar. What had been foreshadowed in the time of Joshua was fulfilled on the first Christian Pentecost, the day of the first universal proclamation, the day when thousands were baptized.

There is a truth at the core of this "preacher's ingenious trick"—the rule of faith confessed at Pentecost had been foreseen, foreordained, and foreshadowed by God since the foundation of the world. Its structure was revealed and foretold in the small details of sacred history.

This method of dividing the creed proved extremely popular, and it dictated the table of contents of many catechisms. Though different readers have divided the "articles" in different ways, they always add up to twelve,

---

[6] Ibid., 39–40.

and it is difficult to imagine a dogma or doctrine of the Church that can't be fit into its categories.

Ingenious indeed.

CHAPTER 9

FATHER FOREVER

WHAT THE PAGANS AND JEWS DENIED—what the Arians and other heretics tried to finesse away—but what the creeds guarded by their words and their very structure—was Christianity's most fundamental and most revolutionary dogma: that God is eternally Father.

It seems today to be an anodyne statement. We take it for granted. The fatherhood of God is one of the foundational teachings of Freemasonry, and Freemasons offer it as a self-evident truth uniting all world religions. "The Fatherhood of God and the Brotherhood of Man" is often carved into the stonework of Masonic temples.

To Westerners (regardless of religious affiliation), God's fatherhood seems an obvious truth independent of Christian Revelation. And that, in itself, is testimony to the success of the Christian creeds.

When non-Christians speak of God as "Father," they are using the word as a metaphor. God stands in relation to creatures as their origin—as a father stands in relation to his children. It is a metaphor because they do not believe that God actually shares the same nature as his creatures. His "fatherhood," as Creator, is temporal, not eternal. It begins in time with his first act of creation.

But that is not what Jesus meant when he addressed God as "Abba! Father!" (Mk 14:36). He was not using a metaphor. He was stating a fact and revealing an eternal truth—the most foundational truth of all.

It was the truth he was willing to die for. It was the truth, in fact, that got him killed.

◆ ◆ ◆

"This was why the Jews sought all the more to kill him, because he not only broke the sabbath but also called God his Father, making himself equal with God" (Jn 5:18).

Jesus' persecutors, it seems, understood the revolutionary implications of his preaching far better than some Christians do. If Jesus claimed to be the Son of God, he was claiming to share God's nature and so to be coequal with his Father. And Jesus' actions bore this out. He claimed superiority to the Jerusalem Temple (Mt 12:5–6), which he said was his "Father's house" (Lk 2:49; Jn 2:16). He made rulings regarding the ancient Law of Moses (Mt 5:21–44). The authorities heard all this and judged it to be blasphemy.

Jesus spoke of a unique, intimate relationship as Son to the Father. He clearly claimed to share divine nature, authority, and power.

Jesus said to them, "Truly, truly, I say to you, the Son can do nothing of his own accord, but only what he sees the Father doing; for whatever he does, that the Son does likewise. For the Father loves the Son, and shows him all that he himself is doing; and greater works than these will he show him, that you may marvel. For as the Father raises the dead and gives them life, so also the Son gives life to whom he will. The Father judges no one, but has given all judgment to the Son, that all may honor the Son, even as they honor the Father. He who does not honor the Son does not honor the Father who sent him. Truly, truly, I say to you, he who hears my word and believes him who sent me, has eternal life; he does not come into judgment, but has passed from death to life.

"Truly, truly, I say to you, the hour is coming, and now is, when the dead will hear the voice of the Son of God, and those who hear will live." (Jn 5:19–25)

Jesus testifies that the Son of God shares everything with the Father. He shares his works, power, authority, and honor and worship. Salvation depends upon this relationship of divine persons.

To be saved is to live in covenant with the God of Jesus Christ. So it is no surprise that Jesus established Baptism "in the name of" the divine persons—Father, Son, and Holy Spirit—and thus established the primordial Christian confession. All later canons, rules, and creeds would be mere elaborations on the baptismal formula.

◆ ◆ ◆

To Jesus' contemporaries, the doctrines of the Trinity and the Incarnation were blasphemous because they seemed to violate God's unity, dignity, and transcendence. How could someone who is "true God"—all-powerful and all-sufficient, wholly other and incomparable—undergo suffering and death? And why would such a God take on a task like that?

Christians believed that the public ministry of Jesus—with his once-for-all, perfect sacrifice—was an image in time of the eternal self-offering of the Son to the Father (see Heb 8–9). Through the sacraments, especially Baptism and Eucharist, Christians entered into the life shared by the Father and Son (see Heb 10:19).

This faith of Christians was not self-evident to the world. St. Paul went so far as to call the content of Christian faith a "stumbling block" to both Jews and pagans (1 Cor 1:23; Gal 5:11). Belief in God *as eternal Father* set Christians apart from everyone else. Belief in Jesus *as eternal Son* was nothing less than a scandal to the first-century world.

Even some early Christians had trouble shaking off the scandal of God's fatherhood. The ancient heresies were marked by a squeamishness about the New Testament's family language. Certain gnostics rejected the revealed terms for God and sought to replace them—with effects that were pretentious and absurd. The wayward priest Valentinus rejected the name "Father," but called instead upon the "First-Beginning . . . First-Unthinkable, who is both unutterable and unnameable."[1] The source for all of his "theology" was, of course, Valentinus himself, whose gnosis—or special knowledge—took precedence over both the Scriptures and the tradition of the Church.

St. Irenaeus punctured Valentinus's doctrine by simply showing it to be arbitrary and idiosyncratic. Since Valentinus felt the freedom to replace divinely revealed terms for God, Irenaeus took Valentinus's terms and replaced them, arbitrarily, with new names such as Gourd, Melon, and Cucumber. It's one of the best bits of comedy in early Christian literature.[2]

Arius, in the fourth century, presented a similar problem. Since he denied the eternity of the Son, he also denied the eternity of God's fatherhood. God cannot be eternally "father" unless he lives eternally in relation with another divine person. And so Arius referred to the deity not as Father, but as "God Unoriginate." Athanasius responded simply by dropping the word "Unoriginate" into the basic Christian prayers:

---

[1] See the quotations in St. Irenaeus of Lyon, *Against Heresies* 1.11.4.

[2] Ibid.

[When Jesus] teaches us to pray, he says not, "When you pray, say, 'O God Unoriginate,'" but rather, "When you pray, say, 'Our Father, which art in heaven.'" And it was his will that the summary of our faith should have the same bearing; so he bid us to be baptized, not into the name of Unoriginate and Originate, nor into the name of Creator and creature, but into the Name of Father, Son, and Holy Spirit. For with such an initiation we too, who are counted as his works, are made sons.[3]

Christianity simply doesn't work when we remove the terms Jesus revealed for the Name of God. Drop in any other terms, and the liturgy makes no sense. The sacraments don't cohere. Salvation becomes a pale reward.

The Gospel, indeed, becomes nonsense.

◆ ◆ ◆

God's fatherhood is revolutionary, and it is essential to the distinctive identity of Christianity. It is what must be confessed for one's faith to be authentic. It is what must be confessed upon entry into the covenant.

The contemporary Protestant theologians Reinhard Feldmeier and Hermann Spieckermann demonstrate this vividly. They note that the Old Testament "characterizes God as Father only seventeen times." In contrast, the

---

[3] St. Athanasius, *Discourses* 1.9.34.

term LORD (YHWH) occurs almost 7,000 times and God (Elohim) about 2,600 times.[4]

With Jesus, however, the religious language takes a radical turn to divine fatherhood. Read carefully the data from the New Testament and the conclusion of these scholars.

> This salutation or designation of God as Father occurs approximately 260 times in the New Testament, not including father metaphors. . . . *The word 'Father' expresses the nature of God in the writings of the New Testament and in the early Christian tradition based on them with an exclusivity unparalleled, to our knowledge, in the history of religions.*[5]

Father. There, in a word, is the Christian revolution. There is the word that set Christianity apart from any religion that has appeared on earth, before or since the birth of Jesus. In the Old Testament, God is presented as Father only rarely, cautiously, and metaphorically. In the New Testament, the terms of divine fatherhood are ubiquitous, prodigal, and metaphysical.

The pattern begun in the Gospels is continued in the Epistles. St. Paul repeatedly begins his letters to the churches: "Grace to you and peace from God our Father"

---

[4] Reinhard Feldmeier and Hermann Spieckermann, *God of the Living: A Biblical Theology* (Waco: Baylor University Press, 2011), 52.

[5] Ibid., emphasis added.

91

(Rom 1:7; see also Gal 1:3; 1 Thess 1:1, etc.). It is his habitual opening because it is his theological starting point. He is not saying that God is somehow "like" a Father. On the contrary, he holds that God is eternally Father because the Word is his eternal Son (see Phil 2:6; Gal 4:4).

As a scholar of the Torah, Paul knew that his usage would be provocative to Jews and pagans alike. In his milieu, it was customary for Jews to call upon God as Father to their nation (see Jn 8:41), but not as Father to an individual. To make such a claim, they assumed, was to make oneself equal with God. For a first-century Jew, the claim of divine sonship was not merely scandalous; it could be a capital offense.

All these thousands of years later, we should still be astonished by Jesus' claim. The theologian Janet Soskice notes: "We should be more startled than we are by the kinship titles in the Bible. Yet . . . kinship titles and related imagery (father, brother, being 'born again') [are] little remarked background noise of Christian speech . . . ordinary language so pervasive as to pass unnoticed."[6]

The doctrine that was scandalous to pagans, Jews, gnostics, and Arians is the doctrine with which the Church has always launched its creeds: I believe in God *the Father*.

---

[6] Janet Martin Soskice, *The Kindness of God: Metaphor, Gender, and Religious Language* (Cambridge: Oxford, 2007), 3.

❖ ❖ ❖

It is a matter of tremendous consequence. Christians in every age have claimed kinship with God through the covenant of Baptism. God is Father to Jesus, and so he is "our Father," too. For in Baptism we are made one with Christ, and the Eucharist strengthens that communion. In the words of a classic formula, we become "sons in the Son"—children of God because we live in the eternal Son of God.[7]

The New Testament is emphatic about this. St. John, after years of preaching, was still startled to proclaim: "See what love the Father has given us, that we should be called children of God; and so we are" (1 Jn 3:1). St. Paul spelled out the consequences of every Christian's incorporation "in Christ."

There is therefore now no condemnation for those who are in Christ Jesus. . . . For all who are led by the Spirit of God are sons of God. For you did not receive the spirit of slavery to fall back into fear, but you have received the spirit of sonship. When we cry, "Abba! Father!" it is the Spirit himself bearing witness with our spirit that we are

---

[7] See *Catechism of the Catholic Church*, 52; Second Vatican Council, Pastoral Constitution on the Church in the Modern World *Gaudium et Spes*, 22; Pope St. John Paul II, General Audience, September 20, 2000; Pope Benedict XVI, General Audience, January 3, 2007; Pope Francis, Homily, Basilica of Saint Paul Outside the Walls, January 25, 2015.

children of God, and if children, then heirs, heirs of God and fellow heirs with Christ.

— Romans 8:1, 14–17

But when the time had fully come, God sent forth his Son, born of woman, born under the law, to redeem those who were under the law, so that we might receive adoption as sons. And because you are sons, God has sent the Spirit of his Son into our hearts, crying, "Abba! Father!" So through God you are no longer a slave but a son, and if a son then an heir.

— Galatians 4:4–7

At the baptismal waters, Christians confess God's fatherhood and then come to share Jesus' sonship. To be saved is not merely to have one's sins forgiven. That is a tremendous gift, but it is preliminary. It is a necessary prerequisite for our divine adoption—the privilege of calling upon God as "Father." We find the idea poetically expressed in the first post-apostolic generation by St. Ignatius of Antioch: "My love has been crucified, and there is no fire in me desiring to be fed; but there is within me a water that lives and speaks, saying to me inwardly, 'Come to the Father.'"[8]

---

[8]   St. Ignatius of Antioch, *Letter to the Romans* 7.

The living water speaks and confesses God as "the Father." With such grace, Ignatius did not fear death and went eagerly to martyrdom rather than abandon his profession of faith.

◆ ◆ ◆

The fatherhood of God. The concept is wallpaper, perhaps, in the neighborhoods where you and I live. Yet it remains a provocation for others and in many places on earth it can still bring down a conviction for blasphemy and even a death sentence.

The doctrine of Islam was fashioned as a reaction against the notion of God's fatherhood. Consider the inscriptions inside the Dome of the Rock, a site revered by Muslims. Constructed during the seventh century, the shrine contains the stone from which, Muslims believe, Mohammed ascended at the end of his earthly days. Inside the dome are colossal inscriptions in Arabic. They are explicitly anti-Trinitarian, taking aim specifically at God's fatherhood and Jesus' sonship.

> The Messiah, Jesus son of Mary, was only a Messenger of God, and his Word which he conveyed unto Mary, and a spirit from him. So believe in God and his messengers, and say not "Three"— Cease! Such is better for you! God is only one God. Far be it removed from his transcendent majesty that he should have a son.

It befits not God that he should take to himself a son.

There is no god but God. He is one. Praise be to God, who has not taken unto himself a son, and who has no partner in sovereignty.

Omar, one of the first and most powerful Caliphs (successors of Mohammed), recalled hearing the Prophet say: "Do not exaggerate in praising me as the Christians praised the son of Mary, for I am only a slave. So call me the slave of Allah and his apostle."[9]

In Islam, God is exclusively transcendent. Thus no one, in heaven or on earth, can call upon God as Father. All other beings stand in relation to God, not as children to a parent, but as slaves to a master. For Mohammed himself, Islam was—most emphatically—submission as a slave, not a son.

The contrast with Christianity could not be more striking. We confess God as Three-in-One, and we believe the Father sent his Son to dwell among us—and share with us the Holy Spirit, so that we, too, might come to know and share divine life. In Jesus, God himself has willed to put aside his transcendence—for us and for our salvation.

We believe that "God is love" (1 Jn 4:8, 16). Note that we do not say that "God loves," but that God *is* love. Love

---

[9] *Hadith* 4:654.

is at the heart of God's identity, because God himself has always had an eternal object of his love. From all eternity, the Father loves the Son, and the Son loves the Father, and the love they share is alive—the Holy Spirit.

The inscriptions in the Dome of the Rock, the traditions of the sayings of Mohammed, and the precedents of Islamic law (*shari'a*) are unanimous in their repudiation of this most fundamental Christian principle.

Islam is hardly unique in this. God's eternal fatherhood cannot be squared any more easily with the other major world religions: Hinduism, Buddhism, Shintoism, Confucianism, or even (as we have seen) Judaism.

Islam is unique, perhaps, in the passion and consistency with which it has imposed this repudiation as a most intolerant form of law.

Only when we understand the revolutionary claims of the creed can we understand why persecutors in the Roman era—and still today—cannot tolerate the simple statement "I am a Christian."

Behind that confession stands a creed. Behind the creed stands a Father whose love, it seems, is so great as to be unimaginable apart from his self-revelation in the Son.

CHAPTER 10

THE CREATOR OF ALL

I RECALL, FROM MY CHILDHOOD in the 1960s, a comedy routine in which a little kid jumps on his bed till it breaks with a loud crash. His dad arrives on the scene within seconds, leaving the boy no time to prepare an excuse. When his dad asks what happened, the boy blames the whole episode on an intruder who came in through the window, jumped on the bed till it broke, and then left, laughing, through the bedroom window.

We all, to some degree, find ourselves in the position of that little boy. We need to account for the messes we've made and the downright evil we find around us. The daily news is full of murder, terrorism, corruption, wars, and rumors of wars. Where does it all come from? Can there really be so many wicked people in the world? And where did their wickedness come from?

Like that little kid, we don't want to blame ourselves. Nor do we really want to blame God.

In the ancient world there arose a religious movement

that sought to blame it all on a malevolent intruder. The movement was called gnosticism.

It wasn't quite Christian or Jewish, though it borrowed many terms and trappings from biblical tradition. It was based on private illumination—*gnosis*, or knowledge—supposedly revealed by God to each individual teacher. As a result, it was as diverse in its doctrine as those teachers. It was always changing and difficult to pin down.

Yet there were certain themes that recurred—and it was against these that the Church's early creeds took careful aim.

Gnostics believed that the problem with the world was the world itself. They judged the material world to be evil to the core, riddled with sicknesses, natural disasters, and everyday disappointments. From all these circumstances they concluded that the world had been created by a malicious demigod. And he fashioned it to be a prison for pure spirits that he trapped in human bodies.[1]

The pure spirits, however, belonged by nature to a realm of light. They belonged to a god—the supreme God—who was far greater than the creator. In some accounts, the lost spirits were "pieces" of God's primordial light, now suffering as they sought a way back to their home beyond the prison of matter.

---

[1] For fuller accounts of gnostic cosmology, see Birger A. Pearson, *Ancient Gnosticism: Traditions and Literature* (Minneapolis: Fortress Press, 2007), 12–14; Kurt Rudolph, *The Nature and History of Gnosticism* (San Francisco: Harper, 1987), 67–76; and Hans Jonas, *The Gnostic Religion* (Boston: Beacon Press, 1963), 43–44.

Many gnostic sects taught that Jesus was the Redeemer sent on a rescue mission by the supreme God. He came to teach the "passwords" the souls needed for the checkpoints along the way out of the universe. He was the spiritual principle opposed to all of material creation. He came not to save the world, but to condemn the world and redeem the exiles who were trapped in it.

Who was the wicked creator god, and where did he come from? Gnostic sects differed about the answer to that question. Some said he was a principle *eternally* opposed to the good God; and so they rendered evil equal to good. Others said the creator was a rebel angel and the universe was the hell he made to torment God's children. The result was always the same: the equation of everything in the world with evil.

Though the gnostics retained some outward appearance of Christianity, they had no use for the tradition of the Apostles. They rejected the Scriptures of Israel, which portrayed creation as "very good" (Gen 1:31). They had no use for the sacraments, which employed material goods—bread, wine, water, and oil—as vessels of divine grace. They repudiated the rule of faith and the creeds, which identified the one true God as the maker of matter.

Against such claims, Christians boldly asserted their belief in one eternal God—not two—who was both Father and Creator. The God who was the origin of human souls was also the maker of human bodies. These were not dueling persons or principles, as the gnostics argued.

Moreover, as Father and Creator, God was almighty—in-vulnerable—and so not subject to harm from rebel angels.

In the words of the creed, God is one, Father, almighty, Creator. Out of nothing God made "all things visible and invisible."

◆ ◆ ◆

To atheists and agnostics, all these distinctions between God and Creator may seem arbitrary and irrelevant. But they have made all the difference in the world. From the orthodox Christian affirmation of the world has come a long tradition of deep reflection on "nature" and creation.

Indeed, Christian belief in the goodness of creation—and rationality of the Creator—has served as the precondition for progress in the empirical sciences. The historian of science Stanley Jaki noted that non-Christian cultures—from the Aztecs to the ancient Chinese—made great discoveries; but none was able to maintain the momentum and develop the sciences in any systematic way. After examining the achievements of Egypt, China, India, Babylon, Greece, and Arabia, he concluded: "in none of those cultures, although they lacked no talent and ingenuity, did science become a self-sustaining enterprise in which every discovery generates another. In all those cultures the scientific enterprise came to a standstill."[2]

---

[2] Stanley L. Jaki, *A Mind's Matter: An Intellectual Autobiography* (Grand Rapids: Eerdmans, 2002), 52.

From the creeds—which summarize the biblical narrative—orthodox Christians learned certain principles that are congenial to science: that everything in creation is totally dependent upon God, who created and sustains it; that the heavens and the earth are ruled by the same laws; and that all physical processes are part of a linear process moving in one direction.

It should not surprise us that so many great scientists in so many various fields were also devout Catholics: St. Albert the Great and Antoine Lavoisier (chemistry), Nicholas Copernicus and Galileo Galilei (astronomy), Blaise Pascal (statistics), Bl. Nicholas Steno (geology and paleontology), Gregor Mendel and Jerome Lejeune (genetics), Louis Pasteur (biology), Georges Lemaitre (cosmology), John von Neumann (computer science), Carlos Chagas Filho and John Eccles (neuroscience), and many of the living winners of the Nobel Prize.

The empirical sciences arose out of Christianity—an orthodox Christianity that was decidedly non-gnostic. Worship of the God of Christianity—the God of Israel—has always involved profound thanksgiving for creation. The world described in Jewish and Christian liturgy is not a prison, but a garden and a sanctuary.

The Psalmist looks at the heavens and earth as the work of God's "fingers," the moon and stars established by God the Creator (Ps 8:3). Within creation, God placed man not as a prisoner, but as steward: "You have given him dominion over the works of your hands; you have put all things under his feet" (Ps 8:6). The heavens tell of God's glory, and their message goes out to all the earth (Ps 19). The human body, too, is not a trap for the spiritual soul, but rather is "wonderfully made" (Ps 139).

◆ ◆ ◆

God is Creator of "all things visible and invisible." Everything in existence has come to be through the will and the creative act of God (Jn 1:3). There are no exceptions. God has no rival, no evil nemesis. Even the angels, though they are mighty by our standards, are merely God's creatures. God's only equal is God, and all power belongs to the Trinity.

Thus there is no place inaccessible to God (Ps 139:7–12), nowhere to run or hide from divine judgment. But, by the same token, there is nowhere from which we cannot be rescued. "God almighty" can conquer even death—and he has.

The opening phrases of the creed establish God's transcendence. He is "other" than everything else we can conceive; for he is the Creator of everything.

Yet the Creator is also "Father," who has made everything for the use and delight of his children. This supreme God, both Father and Creator, will never abandon the righteous to the power of the wicked (Ps 37:33).

It is difficult to imagine a more confident way to begin building a civilization—sciences and all—than to recite the creed. Because so many people believed what they said when they said "Credo," the world, which was already very good, became a much better place.

◆ ◆ ◆

A very important notion in Christian doctrine is the idea of appropriation.

Appropriation is something Christians have always done in speaking of the Trinity. We appropriate to one divine person a quality or action that is "proper" to that person in a special way. For example, we often speak of creation as an attribute—and Creator as a title—as if they belong to the Father alone. Yet we know from Scripture that the Son also was an active agent of creation. In the Acts of the Apostles, St. Peter refers to Jesus as "the author of life" (Acts 3:15). More explicitly, St. John begins his Gospel by saying: "All things were made through [the Word], and without him was not anything made that was made. . . . He was in the world, and the world was made through him" (Jn 1:3, 10). And St. Paul repeatedly refers to Jesus as co-creator with the Father: "For in him all things were created, in heaven and on earth, visible and invisible, whether thrones or dominions or principalities or authorities—all things were created through him and for him" (Col 1:16; see also 1 Cor 8:6). The Letter to the Hebrews affirms that the Father has appointed the Son as "heir of all things, through whom also he created the world" (Heb 1:2).

In appropriating a quality or action to one divine person, we do not exclude the other divine persons. We traditionally speak of the Father as Creator, the Son as Redeemer, and the Holy Spirit as Sanctifier and Consoler. But all three persons participate in creation, all three redeem, and all three sanctify and console.

These qualities and actions are shared. What is *not* shared is the name of each divine person. Only the Father is Father, only the Son is Son, only the Holy Spirit is Holy Spirit. The name represents not what each person does, but who each person is. So the Church does not bless or baptize "in the name of the Creator, Redeemer, and Sanctifier," because those titles are not names. They are titles, but they do not indicate a distinct person in an exclusive way.

This works, in an analogous way, in human society as well. I am a professor, but it does me no good to sign my checks with my job title alone. The bank recognizes only my name.

The creed includes both types of affirmation. It names God as Father, Son, and Holy Spirit, professing belief in each. But it also spells out attributes and actions of each: almighty, creator, judge, giver of life, and so on.

We attribute qualities to each of the Persons, not to the exclusion of the others, but in preference to the others, and we do this based on the evidence we find in Scripture.

The ancient Athanasian Creed employs the principle consistently:

The Father [is] eternal; the Son eternal; and the Holy Ghost eternal. And yet they are not three eternals; but one eternal. As also there are not three uncreated; nor three infinites, but one uncreated; and one infinite. So likewise the Father is Almighty; the Son Almighty; and the Holy Ghost Almighty. And yet they are not three Almighties; but one Almighty.

So we return to our basic terms: Father, almighty, Creator. All of them are important and bear distinctive Christian doctrine. God, almighty, and Creator set orthodoxy apart from gnosticism. They make the world beautiful and make science possible. But only one term—only Father—is a personal name and truly revolutionary.

CHAPTER 11

SON WORSHIP

In a sense the creed is *about* Jesus.

He is the Son of God. He is God the Son. His Incarnation is the event that sets Christian creeds apart from Israel's earlier professions of faith. Every Christian creed, without exception, treats Jesus most extensively of the three divine persons. All of them make precise statements about his divinity, humanity, earthly ministry, redemptive work, and relation to the Father. What the creeds say about the other divine persons, the Father and the Holy Spirit, is simply what Jesus has revealed about them. The creeds mention the Church, at some length, because Jesus himself established it.

Jesus is the complete and perfect revelation of God. Christians have always applied to Jesus the poetic words of Psalm 36:9. Writing in the sixth century, Cassiodorus summed up the tradition of the Fathers: "The verse rightly says of the Savior, 'In your light we shall see light'; that is, the light of the Father and of the Holy Spirit, because through his preaching it happened that the whole Trinity became clear to us."[1]

We could not have known anything about God's inner life if God had not manifested himself so fully by living among us. Jesus made this clear: "All things have been delivered to me by my Father; and no one knows the Son except the Father, and no one knows the Father except the Son and any one to whom the Son chooses to reveal him" (Mt 11:27). A millennium and a half later, St. Francis de Sales said: "We could not successfully contemplate the godhead unless it had been united to the sacred humanity of our Savior."[2]

If we see Jesus, we see God. "He who has seen me has seen the Father" (Jn 14:9). It's important, though, that we see Jesus aright. The creed is like a very clean, very clear, tightly focused lens through which we are sure to see him with accuracy—no filters, no tints, no distortions.

The creed offers us a simple phrase that is true in many different senses: We believe in Jesus Christ. We *believe* in him—that is, we trust him and what he has told us, because only he has the authority to speak to us about God. But we also believe *in* him—that is, we believe because we share his life; we abide in him, and in Jesus we have come to know God's life as if "from the inside."

---

[1] Cassiodorus, *Explanation of the Psalms* 36.10. See also Origen, *On First Principles* 1.1.1, and St. Jerome, *Brief Commentary on the Psalms* 36.

[2] St. Francis de Sales, *Introduction to the Devout Life* (New York: Image, 2003), 71.

◆ ◆ ◆

In its profession of faith in Christ, the Nicene Creed begins with no beginning. Jesus is God's "Only Begotten Son, born of the Father before all ages." Existing before time, he is coeternal with the Father. Through the Prophet Isaiah, YHWH proclaimed:

> Thus says the LORD, the King of Israel
> and his Redeemer, the LORD of hosts:
> "I am the first and I am the last;
> besides me there is no god."
> — Isaiah 44.6

In the Book of Revelation, the same terms are applied to Jesus: "I am the Alpha and the Omega, the first and the last, the beginning and the end" (Rev 22:13; see also 1:17).

What is implicit in Scripture is explicit in the creed. Jesus is pre-existent, coeternal, uncreated: "begotten, not made."

And he is coequal with the Father: God as the Father is God, Light as the Father is Light, and true as the Father is true. What the Father is, the Son is. They share a life and nature so completely that we can unreservedly call them "consubstantial." They share a life and nature so completely that we still profess belief in "one God," though we admit a plurality of divine persons.

Jesus is "Lord," according to the creeds. He is given

the very title, *Kyrios*, that is used in the ancient Greek Septuagint to translate the Hebrew name for God, YHWH. Whatever works were attributed to YHWH in the Old Testament are now attributed also to the Son of God. He is Creator—"through him all things were made." He is Redeemer—"For us men and for our salvation, he came down . . ." As Lord, he rules from heaven, where he has ascended and is enthroned "at the right hand of the Father."

Let there be no doubt: Jesus is God, Lord, Creator (not a creature), and Redeemer (not redeemed). Against the Arians who denied Jesus' divinity, the creed asserts it repeatedly and in a rich variety of terms, using biblical titles, philosophical terminology, and testimonies from the Gospels and Epistles. By marshaling the evidence in one compact statement, the fourth-century creeds make clear the faith the Church had proclaimed since the first century. Writing in 107, St. Ignatius of Antioch, a man already steeped in tradition, repeatedly referred to "Jesus Christ our God."[3]

The creeds boldly proclaim the mystery that rationalists and heretics in every age have denied, from the Arians to the Jehovah's Witnesses, from Mohammed to Thomas Jefferson. "Jesus Christ is Lord" (Phil 2:11).

◆ ◆ ◆

But the Christians who fashioned the creeds took equal pains to demonstrate that Jesus is truly human.

---

[3] See St. Ignatius of Antioch, *Letter to the Ephesians* 1 and 18, *Letter to the Romans* 1.

God the Son could, after all, have simply declared our salvation from heaven, but he did not. Instead, he "came down" and "was incarnate." He was enfleshed. He truly "became man," just as he had always been "true God." He underwent a human birth—from a virgin, the creeds specify. And thus they show that Jesus' origin is with his heavenly Father. His human birth was a real, historical, temporal image of an event that is eternal.

When humans are born, they follow their fathers in temporal sequence. Their fathers must precede them in time. I was born on October 28, 1957, and my eldest son, Michael, was born many years later on December 4, 1982. That's how human begetting works. It's natural.

But Jesus' eternal birth is different and unique. It's supernatural. Since God transcends time and is changeless, the Father and Son are coeternal (and coeternal with the Spirit). Their relationship is one of begetting, but not like my begetting of a son. The Father was always Father, and is always Father, because he is always begetting the Son, the only begotten.

When we recite the creed, then, we are reaching upward, looking upward, from the earthly vantage point selected by God himself.

As Christ was born of the Father before all ages, he is truly divine. Born of a virgin in Bethlehem, he is truly human; yet he remains truly and fully divine.

The creeds, like the Gospels, take pains to give Jesus his proper place—not in myth, but in history. Matthew's

Gospel provides an extensive genealogy, and Luke's is even larger, covering more generations. Luke also names the emperors and governors ruling at key moments in Jesus' life. The Christian story does not take place "once upon a time." It's not a "long time ago in a galaxy far, far away." The Word became flesh at a date that can be ascertained (more or less) and at a spot that can be pinpointed.

So the creeds name names—not only Jesus, but also his mother, Mary, and even the man who condemned Jesus to death, Pontius Pilate.

Pilate was well known from Roman and Jewish sources. His name appears on inscriptions. The Emperor Tiberius assigned him to be the fifth prefect of the province of Judaea, and he definitely made a mark. He was loathed by the Jews who considered him impious and insensitive to their customs. He profaned Jerusalem, the holy city, by raising banners depicting the head of a boar, an unclean animal.

His memory was preserved by his contemporaries and by later historians,[4] almost always in an unflattering light. So Christians gained nothing by including him in the creed—nothing except a marker for historical accuracy. To invoke his name was to make a point about the historicity of Jesus and about history in general. The Word became flesh and dwelt not only among righteous folks, but also with the most notorious and offensive of sinners. Jesus spoke to such sinners of truth and he engaged

---

[4] See, for example, Josephus, *Antiquities of the Jews* 18.3–4.

them in conversation. The Son of God walked into the courtroom of the very regime that would, for centuries, persecute his followers. It was an official of that Roman regime who condemned him to suffer and die. And yet Jesus overcame that death, as would Christians ever after him. Every regime, whatever it may happen to be, presents no lasting threat to Christ or to Christians. Pontius Pilate was feared and resented by his subjects in the first century. Since then, his name is invoked everywhere Christians celebrate the Mass, but not for reasons even remotely related to his own ambitions. Today, on earth, he abides mostly as metadata: a tag for the lifetime of a poor man he condemned to die: Jesus of Nazareth.

The story goes that a keynote speaker canceled, at the last minute, for a parish event. His replacement showed up breathless and began with the line, "Ladies and Gentlemen, I got here the same way Pontius Pilate got into the creed: by accident."

◆ ◆ ◆

With Mary, of course, it is a different story. She got into the creed not by accident, but by willingly receiving the Word. She conceived, the Apostles' Creed tells us, "by the power of the Holy Spirit." Hers was the only human agency involved in Jesus' conception. Thus she is the only believer to be named in the classic Christian creeds. Even in this most minimal account of salvation history she must be named, because salvation turned on her consent—her correspondence to God's will.

Mary's presence in the creed implies so much. As we have already noted, she is the guarantor of Jesus' true humanity and true divinity. But her name in the creed speaks yet another message: it reminds us of our tremendous freedom and dignity. God does not coerce Mary; nor does he coerce us. He does not force his will upon her, but rather awaits her yes, her "Let it be." Nor will he force himself upon us. He establishes the covenant and invites us to live in his family forever; but he does not compel us to accept the terms.

We name Mary in the creed because she is the model of perfect life in covenant with God. Hers is an intelligent obedience and obedient intelligence. She dares to question the angel—not because she doubts him, but because she wants to understand God's plan.

The placement of Mary—even the naming of Mary— is not a late addition in the development of the creeds. She is present in the earliest formulations of the rule of faith. She is named in the creedal summaries of Ignatius, Justin, Irenaeus, and others.

The first Christians found it necessary to invoke her even in these most abbreviated versions of the story of Jesus. Her presence in the creed was for his sake, but also for theirs.

Every creed that invokes Mary names her with a title: "the Virgin." Her virginity, indeed, is essential to the story. But its invocation here has even more significance. For in the ancient world, virginity was considered a shameful condition—something to be mourned (see Judg 11:37-38). A virgin was a woman without the support or protection of a man—and so, typically, a person who was vulnerable and impoverished. A woman's worth was measured by her relationship to a man: her father or her husband or her sons.

With the coming of Christ, such values have been turned on their head. Now the poor are blessed, as are the hungry and persecuted (Lk 6:20-22); and now the virgin is called blessed by all generations (Lk 1:48). In the New Covenant, virginity is a condition of honor, not shame, and many discern it to be their lifelong vocation (see 1 Cor 7).

"*The* Virgin," moreover, is known to be the fulfillment of the Prophet Isaiah's oracle: "Behold, a virgin shall conceive and bear a son, and his name shall be called Emmanuel (which means, God with us)" (Mt 1:23; Is 7:14). Mary's virginity, foreseen and foretold in the Old Covenant, becomes an indisputable testimony to Jesus' status as Messiah, God's anointed, the Christ.

This small point of traditional Christian devotion will always be an essential part of an authentic Christian confession of faith.

◆ ◆ ◆

The Nicene Creed professes not only the fact of God's Incarnation, but also the reason. It was for "our salvation" that the Son of God "came down from heaven." Salvation here has a very specific meaning—a richness that I fear has been lost over the centuries.

When Christians today discuss salvation, they usually speak of it as salvation *from* something. Jesus came, as the Gospel tells us, to "save his people from their sins" (Mt 1:21). That sense is true, and it is wonderful. Nevertheless, it pales in comparison to the full meaning of salvation. For the New Testament makes clear that we are not only saved *from* something; we're also saved *for* something. We're saved for sonship. We're saved so that we might share God's life forever, living as children of God in the eternal Son of God. The forgiveness of sins is a necessary precondition of this, but it's only the beginning.

The Church Fathers, following the New Testament, referred to salvation as a graced exchange. God assumed humanity so that humanity could share his divinity. He "came down from heaven" so that we could go up to heaven with him and live the life he lives. This exchange is a key theme for understanding the letters of St. Paul: "For you know the grace of our Lord Jesus Christ, that though he was rich, yet for your sake he became poor, so that by his poverty you might become rich" (2 Cor 8:9). Elsewhere the Apostle writes: "But when the time had fully come, God sent forth his Son, born of woman, born under the law, to redeem those who were under the law, so that we might receive adoption as sons" (Gal 4:4–5).

This is the deepest meaning of salvation: through Baptism we become "partakers of the divine nature" (2 Pet 1:4). When the early Fathers spoke of redemption, they dared to describe it with terms such as *theosis* and *theopoiesis*—divinization and deification.[5]

If God had merely saved us from sins, it would be enough. In fact, it would be the greatest gift imaginable. Instead, however, he chose to surpass the limits of our imagination when he "came down from heaven" to save us. Not only did he make himself like us—and not only did he save us from our sins—but he made us like himself. Here is how St. Athanasius put the matter in the years between the Council of Nicaea and the Council of Constantinople: "For he was made man that we might be made God," and "he himself has made us sons of the Father, and deified men by becoming himself man."[6]

It is an axiom of philosophy that knowledge depends on a certain similarity between the knower and the known. I can know you because we share a common human nature. I can know cheese because it's a material substance, as I am, and it's made up of carbon, hydrogen, and oxygen, as I am, and so on.

But God is not like us—or like anything else that we know. He is entirely *other*—the Creator who transcends

---

[5] For an extensive treatment of the biblical and patristic doctrine, see Daniel A. Keating, *Deification and Grace* (Naples: Sapientia Press, 2007). See also Michael J. Christensen and Jeffery A. Wittung, eds., *Partakers of the Divine Nature: The History and Development of Deification in the Christian Traditions* (Grand Rapids: Baker, 2007).

[6] St. Athanasius of Alexandria, *On the Incarnation of the Word* 54.3.

all creation. We know of him only what he has revealed in his mercy. Yet, in his mercy he has revealed himself entirely in Jesus Christ. In his mercy God has given us—as an unmerited grace—similarity with himself. Through Christ and in Christ, we come to know the Son by living his life—the life of a child of God.

We are deified. Divinized. What else could Jesus have meant when he quoted the Psalm and said, "You are gods" (Jn 10:34; Ps 82:6)? What else could the Second Letter of Peter mean by the outrageous claim that we are "partakers of the divine nature" (2 Pet 1:4)?

We can know God because he has become like us—and because he has made us like himself. Apart from Jesus we could never come to know eternity or divinity. They are utterly alien to us. And we certainly could never be called what we now are: *children of God* (1 Jn 3:1). St. John describes this interpersonal knowledge between us and God in profound and poetic terms.

That which was from the beginning, which we have heard, which we have seen with our eyes, which we have looked upon and touched with our hands, concerning the word of life—the life was made manifest, and we saw it, and testify to it, and proclaim to you the eternal life which was with the Father and was made manifest to us—that which we have seen and heard we proclaim also to you, so that you may have fellowship with us;

and our fellowship is with the Father and with his Son Jesus Christ.

— 1 John 1:1–3

We are saved for fellowship—the Greek word is *koinonia*, communion! We are saved in order to be united with Christ. We are saved so that we can call God "Our Father."

Such salvation depends upon the truth of Jesus' divinity. As St. Athanasius said: "Man would not have been deified if joined to a creature, if the Son had not been true God."[7] But salvation depends also upon the truth of Jesus' humanity. If the Son's Incarnation had been an illusion—a "seeming," as the heretics said—then it would have been void of any saving power. "What has not been assumed has not been healed," said St. Gregory of Nazianzus.[8]

Athanasius was the custodian of the legacy of Nicaea, and Gregory was the genius behind Constantinople, the second council that shaped our Sunday creed. If we want to be true to the faith they expressed, we need to know what they meant in their expressions. Jesus "came down" "for our salvation," and that salvation was far more than a rescue mission. It was a New Covenant, the establishment of a real family bond between us and God, almighty and eternal.

---

[7] St. Athanasius, *Discourses Against the Arians* 2.70.
[8] St. Gregory of Nazianzus, *Letters* 101.32.

Like God's fatherhood, our adoption is not a metaphor. It is real. Pope St. John Paul II saw this as supremely good news: "We are not the sum of our weaknesses and failures," he said. "We are the sum of the Father's love for us and our *real* capacity to become the image of his Son."[9]

◆ ◆ ◆

We become more godlike as we strive to imitate God's human life. That is why we rehearse a brief summary of that life whenever we recite the creed.

Many people find it strange that the creed skips from Jesus' birth immediately to his suffering on Good Friday. Isn't it odd that we don't mention his baptism, his miracles, or his sermons? But no: in one line he's born of the Virgin Mary and in the next line he's crucified under Pontius Pilate.

In this the creeds are somewhat like the Gospels. In 1892 the German scholar Martin Kähler described Mark's Gospel as "a passion narrative with extended introduction."[10]

The truth is that the events of Jesus' final Passover—what tradition calls the Paschal Mystery—mark the culmination of our salvation. Everything else Jesus said and did was simply preparation for that moment, when he died and rose and took his place in glory.

---

9   St. Pope John Paul II, Homily, World Youth Day, Toronto, July 28, 2002. Emphasis added.

10   Martin Kähler, *The So-Called Historical Jesus and the Historic, Biblical Christ* (1892; reprint, Philadelphia: Fortress, 1964), 80.

Most of us will not have an opportunity to imitate Jesus' miracles. We won't be called upon to multiply loaves or fishes. We won't be asked to cure blindness or leprosy. We will, however, probably suffer much before we leave this earthly life. And we will certainly die.

In his suffering, Jesus taught us how to suffer. He showed us how to suffer. But, more than that, by his communion with us he *enables* us to suffer as he did. He *endows* our suffering with salvific power. St. Paul suffered horribly—everything from beatings and floggings to prison and shipwreck—and yet he could say with perfect honesty: "Now I rejoice in my sufferings for your sake, and in my flesh I complete what is lacking in Christ's afflictions for the sake of his body, that is, the Church" (Col 1:24).

Christ lived in Paul, and so suffered in Paul. "It is no longer I who live," the Apostle said, "but Christ who lives in me; and the life I now live in the flesh I live by faith in the Son of God, who loved me and gave himself for me" (Gal 2:20).

Suffering is an inevitable part of human life; but *salvific* suffering is a power available only to those who live in communion with Christ. It is available only to the divinized, the children of God alive in the eternal Son.

No pain need be pointless. No suffering should be wasted. When we experience these passions, we are sharing Christ's Passion. We are sharing his Paschal Mystery. Thus we are more perfectly living the life into which we are baptized. We are more perfectly embodying the faith of the creed.

Of course, neither the Gospels nor the creed end the story with Jesus' death. The Resurrection follows, as does his Ascension into glory, with the promise of his return. The creed reminds us of all these events, and reminds us also that our faith has a future tense. We look to the future with hope because "he will come again in glory" as judge and will establish a never-ending kingdom. Because he has already conquered every enemy—even death!—we know that he can fulfill these promises, and we don't hesitate to profess them as essentials of the faith.

◆ ◆ ◆

"When I am weak," said St. Paul, "then I am strong" (2 Cor 12:10).

The creed seems repeatedly to require our belief in things that cannot be proven. It seemed crazy to pagans that Christians worshipped a man. It seemed the height of absurdity that they worshipped a crucified man—who had undergone this most humiliating punishment at the command of a Roman governor of mediocre accomplishments.

Yet these were the mysteries that Christians professed whenever they stood to recite the creed. They led with the most difficult matters, and they spoke of them not vaguely but with intensifying precision.

They spoke of Jesus—not as a wisdom teacher. In fact, they repeated none of his proverbs. They spoke of him not as a wonderworker. They spoke of nothing "except Jesus Christ and him crucified" (1 Cor 2:2).

And as long as they did so, Christians endured. The Marcionites edited out the inconvenient parts of the Gospels, and they faded away from the impotence of their message. The gnostics rationalized every seeming paradox, and they perished of irrelevance. The docetists, Arians, and countless others died off—not from persecution, but from the anemia of their creedless counsels.

The Church of the creeds, on the other hand, was persecuted and put to death, and yet it has persevered, endured, and triumphed. Because it worships Christ, it is one with him, it is like him, and it knows him.

CHAPTER 12

THAT'S THE SPIRIT

Councils often represent the *beginning* of a resolution
to a particular crisis in the Church. Alas, the fixes are rarely quick. A creed is not a cure-all. And the bishops who
were triumphant in council chamber do not necessarily
return to their sees as heroes.

The orthodox arguments won the day at Nicaea, but
the Arian heresy was hardly vanquished. Many authorities in Church and state remained Arian and continued
to promote the cause. And the heresy itself metastasized
into many "semi-Arian" forms that eluded censure even as
they perpetuated error.

In the generation after the council, some theologians
had begun to repurpose the old Arian arguments in a new
form. Instead of arguing against the coeternity and co-
equality of the Father and Son, they directed their argument against the deity of the Holy Spirit. As a movement,
the trend was not very cohesive, and it never produced a
champion as savvy as Arius. An early leader, Macedonius,
actually came to be named bishop in Constantinople, but

he was little loved and held office only briefly before the emperor had him deposed.

The phenomenon went by different names in different regions. The orthodox Fathers tended to lump its various manifestations into the category *Pneumatomachian*, which means "those who make war against the Spirit."

It was a weaker movement than Arianism had been. Perhaps potential allies were deterred by Jesus' words: "And whoever says a word against the Son of man will be forgiven; but whoever speaks against the Holy Spirit will not be forgiven, either in this age or in the age to come" (Mt 12:32; see also Mk 3:29 and Lk 12:10).

Still, it gained ground, largely because the most eloquent defenders of Nicaea had been neutralized. St. Athanasius learned about the movement against the Spirit's deity when he was living underground—hiding in the desert during his third exile from Alexandria. There he received a letter from his friend Serapion of Thmuis, who told of an alarming number of Christians who claimed that the Nicene faith was perfectly compatible with belief that the Holy Spirit was a creature (perhaps an angel).

Athanasius saw that Pneumatomachianism was Arianism repackaged and repurposed—now directed at the third person rather than the second person of the Trinity. The effect was the same: a religion that was vaguely unitarian, and the denial of worship to any but the supreme solitary God, whom we know as "the Father," but whose fatherhood is not eternal. Those who made war on the Spirit also made war on the common understanding of salvation. If the Spirit Christians received at Baptism was not truly divine, then they were not truly divinized.

Athanasius replied with history's first treatise devoted entirely to the Holy Spirit, his justly famous *Letter to Serapion*. Others soon followed, works by St. Basil the Great, Didymus the Blind, and St. Gregory of Nazianzus.

Treatises helped. They showed the elites at least that the case for the coeternal, coequal Trinity was scriptural, traditional, and sound. But the orthodox position remained vulnerable because the established creeds, including that of Nicaea, gave the Holy Spirit little more than a mention.

This crisis, like the earlier Arian crisis, would require its own council and a fuller creed.

◆ ◆ ◆

The council for this crisis would take place in 381 in Constantinople. We know little about the proceedings. We do know that the Pneumatomachian bishops were denied entry when they refused to recite the Nicene Creed. They could not bring themselves to affirm even that barest minimum: "I believe . . . in the Holy Ghost." The original Nicene Creed said no more, and ended there, rather abruptly.

Led by St. Gregory of Nazianzus, the most revered of the Eastern Fathers, the Council of Constantinople expanded the article on the Holy Spirit, making quite clear that the Holy Spirit is divine.

> I believe in the Holy Spirit, the Lord, the giver of life,
> who proceeds from the Father,
> who with the Father and the Son is adored and
>   glorified,
> who has spoken through the prophets.

The Spirit, like Jesus and like YHWH in the Old Testament, is Lord.

The Spirit, again like the other divine persons, does what only God can do: give life (see Deut 32:39).

Thus, the Spirit enjoys all the prerogatives that belong exclusively to God. Like the Father and Son—"with the Father and Son"—the Spirit "is adored and glorified."

These are bold additions to the Nicene formula, but every assertion rests squarely on scriptural foundations. St. Paul calls the Spirit "Lord" (2 Cor 3:17–18) and speaks of the Spirit as glorified and giving glory. Jesus himself revealed that the Spirit is the giver of life (John 6:63), which Paul affirms as well (2 Cor 3:6). Jesus also speaks of the Spirit's procession from the Father (Jn 15:26). St. Peter and St. Luke both testify that the Spirit has spoken through the prophets (2 Pet 1:21 and Acts 28:25).

That the Spirit should be adored we know from the concluding chapters of the Book of Revelation. There John gives us a stunning poetic image of the Trinity in heaven: "Then he showed me the river of the water of life, bright as crystal, flowing from the throne of God and of the Lamb" (Rev 22:1). The Father appears as "God," the Son as the Lamb, and the Spirit as the river of life-giving water. This image in Revelation is a clear fulfillment of Jesus' promise in John 7:37–39:

> On the last day of the feast, the great day, Jesus stood up and proclaimed, "If anyone thirst, let him come to me and drink. He who believes in me, as the scripture has said, 'Out of his heart shall flow rivers of living water.'" Now this he said about the Spirit, which those who believed in him were to receive.

◆ ◆ ◆

The line is worth repeating: "This he said about the Spirit, which those who believed in him were to receive." Jesus issues his invitation to "anyone" who thirsts for salvation. To those who believe he promises salvation through the gift of the Spirit.

Thus he presents the gift of the Spirit as the culminating mystery of redemption. Recall that (in the words of the creed) Jesus "came down from heaven" "for our salvation." And the Fathers understood salvation as the Christian's share in divine life. In this passage from St. John's Gospel, Jesus makes clear that divine life is given to us *as the Holy Spirit.*

What is first in intention, then, is last in execution. The giving of the Holy Spirit is the reason for the Incarnation. Pentecost is the reason for Christmas and Good Friday and Easter and the Ascension. Throughout his earthly ministry, Jesus longed to light a fire upon the earth (Lk 12:49), and only on Pentecost—with the appearance of the Spirit as tongues of flame (Acts 2:3)—do we see that fire blazing.

It is only by the Spirit that we can know God: "For what person knows a man's thoughts except the spirit of the man which is in him? So also no one comprehends the thoughts of God except the Spirit of God" (1 Cor 2:11). It is only by the Spirit that we can pray as children of God and not as slaves: "For you did not receive the spirit of slavery to fall back into fear, but you have received the spirit of sonship. When we cry, 'Abba! Father!'" (Rom 8:15; see also Gal 4:6). It is in the Spirit that we live (Rom 8:9) and are baptized (1 Cor 6:11) and become a dwelling place for God (Eph 2:22). It is in the Spirit that God is revealed to us (Rev 1:10).

The scriptural testimony to the life and missions of the Holy Spirit is abundant. It is a wonder that the Council of Nicaea gave so little space to the Spirit in its final article. Indeed, less than a century afterward, St. Augustine complained, "Many books have been written by scholarly and spiritual men on the Father and the Son. . . . The Holy Spirit has, on the other hand, not yet been studied with as much care and by so many great and learned commentators."[1] And little has changed over seventeen centuries. Pope Francis remarked, quite recently, that "the Holy Spirit is unknown!"[2] His immediate predecessor observed that "the Holy Spirit has largely remained the Unknown God."[3]

It is a circumstance we should want to remedy, even after millennia of precedent. Yet Cardinal Ratzinger helps us to understand, perhaps, why even a great creed-making ecumenical council could come to exemplify this "neglect." He notes that the Spirit—in all of Sacred Scripture—never testifies to the Spirit, but rather only to the Father and to the Son. Thus we know the Spirit only by the fire cast upon the earth. We know the Spirit by divine deeds. Cardinal Ratzinger concludes: "We can never know the Spirit otherwise than in what he accomplishes. This is why Scripture never describes the Spirit in himself. It tells us only how he comes to man and how he can be distinguished from other spirits."[4]

When the Church recites the creed received from the Council of Constantinople—the creed we today call "Nicene"—we confess more about the Holy Spirit than in the Apostles' creed or in the creed that was actually produced at Nicaea. We speak of the Spirit's eternal life and earthly mission. And yet we never transgress the divine

---

[1] St. Augustine of Hippo, *On the Faith and the Creed*, 9.18–19.

[2] Pope Francis, "The Unknown Holy Spirit," Morning Meditation in the Chapel of the Domus Sanctae Marthae, Monday, May 13, 2013.

[3] Joseph Ratzinger, *The God of Jesus Christ* (San Francisco: Ignatius Press, 2008), 105.

[4] Ibid., 109.

modesty that is proper to the third person of the Trinity. The council Fathers, it seems, had a precise sense of exactly how far to go—far enough to correct errors, far enough to instill devotion, yet not so far as to eclipse the primary revelation of God's fatherhood.

◆ ◆ ◆

In the years immediately following the Council of Nicaea, churches throughout the world began to adapt the Nicene Creed for use in the Rite of Baptism. Some churches called upon the officiating clergy to recite each line, which would then be repeated by the candidate for Baptism. Others rendered the articles of the creed in question-and-answer form. All of these were known under the umbrella title "the faith of Nicaea." The creed of the Council of Constantinople was quite likely assembled from these various forms.

And there may have been further variations after Constantinople. The oldest reference we have to the creed of Constantinople is in the canons of the Council of Chalcedon, seventy years later, in 451. What the Fathers of Chalcedon presented was the faith of the Fathers of Constantinople, symbolized by the creed. The faith of Constantinople was the faith of Nicaea, which was the faith of the Apostles. In the acts of the Council of Ephesus (431) we find a similar reverence for sacred tradition: "The holy Synod decreed that it is unlawful for any man to bring forward, or to write, or to compose a different faith as a rival to that established by the holy Fathers assembled with the Holy Spirit in Nicaea."[5]

The creed had changed at Constantinople, but the faith it represented was unchanging and unchangeable.

It would change again, though only slightly and almost exclusively in the Western Church. In the sixth century, Christians in Spain took up the practice of singing the creed at every Sunday Mass. They used a text that added a single word, *Filioque* (meaning "and the Son"), in the line about the Holy Spirit's procession. Instead of saying that the Spirit "proceeds from the Father," the Spaniards' text said that the Spirit "proceeds from the Father and the Son." The practice spread throughout the Latin churches and was almost universal in the West by the year 1100.

It was an alteration to the creed, but it was certainly not a doctrinal innovation. The Latin Fathers had always used the language of the double procession. There are instances in Tertullian in the second century and Marius Victorinus in the fourth. It is a major theme in St. Augustine's book *On the Trinity* and it is upheld by later Fathers, including Pope St. Leo the Great and, one of the greatest of the Eastern Fathers, St. Maximus the Confessor.[6] A similar formula—indicating that the Spirit proceeds from the Father through the Son—appears in

---

[5] Council of Ephesus, canon 7.

[6] For a full treatment of the ancient witnesses, see Avery Dulles, S.J., "The *Filioque*: What Is at Stake," *Concordia Theological Quarterly* (January–April 1995): 31–48. Also see Michael D. Torre, "John Damascene and St. Thomas Aquinas on the Eternal Procession of the Holy Spirit," *St. Vladimir's Theological Quarterly* 38 (1994): 303–27.

the works of other Eastern Fathers: St. Gregory of Nyssa, St. Epiphanius of Cyprus, St. Ephrem of Syria, St. Cyril of Alexandria, and St. John of Damascus. So the notion of a double procession was hardly a provincial peculiarity. By the end of the patristic era, it appears, in one or another variant, in important works by great saints and teachers in almost every corner of the world.

In the ninth century, however, the Patriarch of Constantinople, Photius, numbered the addition of the *Filioque* among his many grievances against the West as he led his see into schism. He went further in charging that the *Filioque* represented not merely a liturgical innovation, but a heretical doctrine.

It would be difficult to square the charge of heresy with the witness of so many saints, from both the Eastern and Western traditions. But it is difficult as well to square the charge with Scripture. Some years ago, Cardinal Avery Dulles examined the texts most often invoked by saints and theologians. He concluded, modestly:

> Admittedly we do not have any New Testament text which teaches formally that the Spirit proceeds from the Son, but a number of texts, read in convergence, seem to imply this. John 5:19, for example, says that the Son does only what He sees the Father doing—a statement which seems to refer to the externally existing Son and hence to imply that the Son, together with the Father,

breathes forth the Spirit. In John 16:14 Jesus says that the Spirit of Truth will take from the Son what is the Son's and declare it to the believing community. This "taking" is often understood as referring to the procession. Then again, in the Revelation to John, the river of the water of life is said to flow from the throne of God and of the Lamb (Revelation 22:1). Read in conjunction with Ezekiel 36:25–26, John 3:5, John 4:10, and 1 John 5:6–8, this river of living water may be understood as the life-giving Spirit.

What is merely suggested by these texts is impressively confirmed by the titles given to the Spirit in the New Testament. He is repeatedly called the Spirit of the Son (Galatians 4:6), the Spirit of Jesus (Acts 16:7), the Spirit of the Lord (2 Corinthians 3:17), the Spirit of Christ (1 Peter 1:11), and the Spirit of Jesus Christ (Philippians 1: 19).[7]

The New Testament texts bear out the principle we examined in Chapter 8: through the *economy* the *theology* is revealed to us. God's actions in time—in history, in creation and redemption—reveal something about his nature. *What God does* reflects *who he is.* In the Gospels, the Father sends the Son, and the Son sends the Spirit. Jesus breathes on the Apostles and tells them to "Receive

---

[7] Dulles, S.J., "The *Filioque*: What Is at Stake," 38–39.

the Holy Spirit" (Jn 19:22). From this we learn of eternal love. The Father's love is generative: it generates a perfect image of himself (Col 1:15). The Son's love for the Father is equal to the Father's love for the Son; and the love they share is a Person, the Holy Spirit. Thus, St. Augustine and other saints appropriated divine love in a particular way to the Holy Spirit, precisely because the Spirit proceeds from mutual love of the Father and the Son.[8]

Nevertheless, the accusations of Photius have only gained momentum down the years, exacerbated by political divisions, linguistic differences, and cultural prejudices. The schism of Photius was reprised in the eleventh century, and the rhetoric has only grown more ferocious in the Orthodox East. Yet the eminent Orthodox theologian David B. Hart, after analyzing the data, dismisses the charge out of hand. He writes:

I can think of no better example of an almost entirely imaginary theological problem, pursued with ferocious pertinacity solely because it serves to exaggerate and harden—or, rather, to rationalize—the division between Christian East and West, but that succeeds only in distorting the tradition of both almost beyond recognition.[9]

---

[8] For a full catalogue of Augustine's texts related to the theology and economy of the Spirit's procession, see the article "Holy Spirit" in Allan D. Fitzgerald, O.S.A., editor, *Augustine through the Ages: An Encyclopedia* (Grand Rapids: Eerdmans, 1999), 434–437.

[9] David B. Hart, "The Myth of Schism," in Francesca A. Murphy and Christopher Asprey, eds., *Ecumenism Today: The Universal Church in the 21st Century*

Hart goes on to demonstrate how the logic of anti-*Filioque* polemics can be turned against Orthodox theology of the Holy Spirit as well—and indeed against the theological enterprise. Addressing one common anti-*Filioque* line of argument, he concluded:

> This is theologically disastrous, and in fact subversive of the entire Eastern patristic tradition of Trinitarian dogma. Were this claim sound, there would be absolutely no basis for Trinitarian theology at all; the arguments by which the Cappadocians defended full Trinitarian theology against Arian and Eunomian thought . . . would entirely fail. Orthodoxy would have no basis whatsoever.[10]

I don't want to engage in a counter-polemic, or even a full-scale defense. This is not the place. The Holy See, in any event, has given the Eastern Churches in communion with Rome permission to drop the phrase in liturgical use. When the popes pray with prelates from the Christian East, the phrase is customarily omitted. The Western Church, I believe, has conceded as much as it can, since the double procession is a doctrine that runs deep in tradition.

(Burlington: Ashgate, 2008), 98–99.

[10] Ibid., 100.

❖ ❖ ❖

According to St. Augustine, the Holy Spirit is the bond of love uniting the Father and the Son. The Spirit is the love shared by the Father and Son. Similarly, the Spirit is the bond of love—the covenant bond—that unites Christians with Jesus Christ. St. Paul spelled this out as he wrote about the New Covenant to the Church in Corinth: "Our competence is from God," he explained, "who has made us competent to be ministers of a new covenant, not in a written code but in the Spirit; for the written code kills, but the Spirit gives life" (2 Cor 3:5–6).

The Spirit is the life of the covenant, the life of God's family on earth. It is as the Lord said—as was "spoken through the prophets":

And as for me, this is my covenant with them, says the LORD: my spirit which is upon you, and my words which I have put in your mouth, shall not depart out of your mouth, or out of the mouth of your children, or out of the mouth of your children's children, says the LORD, from this time forth and for evermore.

— Isaiah 59:21

CHAPTER 13

THE CHURCH AND THE FUTURE

THE FIRST COUNCIL OF CONSTANTINOPLE, which expanded the creedal treatment of the Holy Spirit, gave us still more. It gave the creed a concluding section on the Church. What had formerly been merely a drive-by mention ("I believe in the Holy Spirit, the holy Catholic Church, the communion of saints . . .") now became a rather detailed confession about the particular qualities of the Church of Jesus Christ.

> I believe in one, holy, catholic and apostolic
>   Church.
> I confess one Baptism for the forgiveness of sins
> and I look forward to the resurrection of the dead
> and the life of the world to come. Amen.

Because of the nature of the council, many commentators do not treat this material separately, but rather as part of the preceding material on the Holy Spirit. There is something to be said for that approach. The Holy Spirit, as St. Augustine said, is the soul of the Church.[1] The Church is not born until God pours his Spirit out upon the disciples gathered in Jerusalem. Yes, the Church is the Body of Christ, but the Spirit given to the Church is the "Spirit of Jesus" (Phil 1:19), the "Spirit of Christ" (Rom 8:9; 1 Pet 1:11). The triune God cannot be divided, though the three persons can be distinguished. The Church belongs to the Holy Spirit in the most profound sense.

Yet it is helpful also to give focused consideration to the Church, and I believe that was the intention of the Fathers as they framed these final words of the creed. For the first councils—Nicaea, Constantinople, Ephesus, Chalcedon—were summoned precisely because of divisions in the Church and disputes about the faith of the Church. Bound up in these concluding words is the identity—with identifying marks—of the covenant People of God. Bound up in these concluding words is the *authority to impose such words*, the authority to make a creed, which only the Church can do.

◆ ◆ ◆

In my book *Reasons to Believe* I have made an extensive study of the New Testament roots of the four "marks of the Church"; and in this book I've provided the key

---

[1]   See St. Augustine of Hippo, *Sermons* 267.4. See also the discussion in Charles Cardinal Journet, *The Theology of the Church* (San Francisco, CA: Ignatius Press, 2004), 83–89.

scriptural passages for the four marks in Appendix B, "A Biblical Creed." Entire libraries can be written (and have been written) on this article of the creed, as on all the others. Here I hope to make just a few points relative to our theme of "creed and covenant."

◆ ◆ ◆

Is it right to think of the Church as an object of our faith? The creed asks us to *believe in* the Father, the Son, and the Holy Spirit—and then it presents a further test. Then it asks us to profess our faith in the Church.

Ultimately, of course, God is the one in whom we must put all of our faith, hope, and love. But we know that God calls us to love others for the love of him. We know also that Christ established the Church to be "the pillar and bulwark of truth" (1 Tim 3:15). And, furthermore, he identified himself inseparably with the Church (Acts 9:4). The Church is his Body on earth (1 Cor 12:27, Eph 5:23, Col 1:18).

This close identification of God with his covenant family, his "household" on earth, is not self-evident to our senses and so it is properly an object of faith. Yet the identity of the Church is not a secret, either, and the New Testament clearly identifies it by certain qualities or marks, and distinguishes it from its would-be rivals. The Church is visible, but it is something more than meets the eye. There is something supernatural about the Church. Otherwise it would not be in the creed.

St. Paul expressly calls the Church a mystery (Eph 3:8–10). In fact, the mystery of the Church is so great, he goes on to say, that the principalities and powers, the angels in heaven, learn the wisdom of God from the Church!

Thus, while we know that the Church has a human element, we know also that it has a divine element, a supernatural reality.

What enables us to see the supernatural truth of the Church so clearly is not our intelligence, but rather the faith that is a gift from God. Our faith is, from beginning to end, a grace. Think of the most beautiful stained-glass cathedral windows and how different they appear, depending on where you're standing. Stand outside, and the windows appear to be a meaningless mass of lead and dull colors. Stand inside, and their beautiful colors and vibrant designs captivate you.

The higher truth of the Church is like that. The reason for the difference is the light of faith. This scandal, this stumbling block, is an extension of the same scandal that Jesus presented two thousand years ago. A bystander might see a thirty-three-year-old Palestinian Jew with incredible and extraordinary wonderworking powers, while Peter would see the Son of the Living God.

When Simon Peter confessed what he saw, Jesus answered him, "Blessed are you, Simon Bar-Jona! For flesh and blood has not revealed this to you, but my Father who is in heaven" (Mt 16:17). Jesus called upon him to confess what he could not have known apart from the gift of faith. Such is the truth the Church confesses in the creed.

◆ ◆ ◆

When we confess the Church along with the supernatural realities, we are beholding the masterpiece of Christ. We're not saying that what Christ did wasn't enough; we're looking at the fullness of the finished work of Christ, which is not reducible to individualistic experience or simple fellowships of like-minded and like-experienced Christians.

The Church is what Christ has made it. It is the family of God. It is the New Covenant. It is the Body of Christ.

And, as a body is one, so the Church is one. Jesus promised: "I have other sheep, that are not of this fold; I must bring them also, and they will heed my voice. So there shall be one flock, one shepherd" (Jn 10:16). Later in the same Gospel, Jesus prays: "Holy Father, keep them in thy name, which thou hast given me, that they may be one, even as we are one" (Jn 17:11).

Jesus' oneness with the Father is eternal, invisible, and spiritual. Yet it is also physical and visible. His Incarnation made it so. In a similar way, the Incarnation dramatically transformed the reality of the People of God. He identifies with them in a visible way, in a true communion. Because the Father made the Son visible and physical, so the Body of Christ is visible and physical and one with a supernatural unity that comes ultimately from the Trinity.

The unity itself is not always visible because of the counter-witness of those who profess the faith but live lives full of hatred and lies. But Christ prayed that the Church would be one, and we believe that the Father answers his prayer. The Church receives the grace. Yet we must be exhorted and we must strive to correspond to it. St. Paul told the Corinthians: "I appeal to you, brethren, by the name of our Lord Jesus Christ, that all of you agree and that there be no dissensions among you, but that you be united in the same mind and the same judgment" (1 Cor 1:10). Visible Christian unity, it seems, is a work in progress.

Meanwhile, the supernatural bond of unity holds together in one divine, Mystical Body people who are Australian, African, Asian, European, and American. That is the work of Christ.

Israel, in reciting the Shema, always confessed God's oneness. The Church confesses that God's oneness now, in the New Covenant, extends as well to the Church, his covenant family. "There is one body and one Spirit . . . one Lord, one faith, one baptism, one God and Father of us all, who is above all and through all and in all" (Eph 4:4–6).

Still, the New Covenant follows the pattern established in the Old. In the Old Testament covenants, God called upon one mediator (Noah, Abraham, Moses, David) and one family (Noah's household, Abraham's tribe, Israel's confederation of tribes, David's kingdom). Apart from that one mediator, apart from that one family, there was no access to the covenant—and so, no ordinary means of salvation (see, for example, Heb 11:7; 1 Pet 3:20; and 2 Pet 2:5).

◆ ◆ ◆

Because the Church is Christ's Body it is holy. How could it be otherwise? Its holiness is visible in the earthly lives of the saints—those who are canonized and those whom we know from ordinary life. They imitate Christ as well as they can with God's grace. They participate in his actions. They are "God's co-workers" (1 Cor 3:9) and can say with St. Paul: "I complete what is lacking in Christ's afflictions for the sake of his body, that is, the Church" (Col 1:24).

To live in this way is to be holy. It is to live as a child of God—with the life of the eternal Son of God—not just later in heaven, but even now on earth. When Catholics sing the ancient hymn of the Gloria they speak the truth to Almighty God: "You alone are the holy one." Only God is holy. Yet he has, in his mercy, chosen to share his holiness with the people in his covenant family, the Church. St. Paul dares to speak of Church members as "the saints"—"the holy ones" (see, for example, 1 Cor 14:33, Eph 1:1).

Christians are holy by means of the Baptism at which they profess the creed. "For as many of you as were baptized into Christ have put on Christ" (Gal 3:27). Holiness is a grace administered by the Church and given to God's children, as they become a "new creation" through the New Covenant Rites of Initiation. St. Paul sets these rites apart from the initiation that foreshadowed them: "For neither circumcision counts for anything, nor uncircumcision, but a new creation" (Gal 6:15). With Baptism comes a new rule of faith and the right to claim the name of God's covenant family: "Peace and mercy be upon all who walk by this rule, upon the Israel of God" (Gal 6:16).

The Israel of God permits no divisions by ethnicity or geography. The Church is one as it is holy, and God accomplishes both unity and sanctity by means of the Church's sacraments: "But now in Christ Jesus you who once were far off have been brought near in the blood of Christ. For he is our peace, who has made us both one, and has broken down the dividing wall of hostility" (Eph 2:13–14).

God himself, in Christ, has broken down the wall that had, since Adam, separated people from sharing in his holiness. In the Old Covenant he restricted the human share in that holiness to the tabernacle, the Temple, and the worship of Israel. But in Christ we have one "greater than the Temple" (Mt 12:6), and in his Church the very "Israel of God."

◆ ◆ ◆

But which Church is this? Already in the first century there were multiple claimants to the title. It was against them that St. Ignatius of Antioch, at the turn of the second century, invoked the authority of the "Catholic Church."[2] There was already, even then, a Church recognizable from city to city, province to province, and continent to continent. Ignatius did not adapt his material to suit differing theologies in Smyrna and Rome. In each place he assumed that the Church looked the same; it had the same hierarchical structure of bishop, presbyter, and deacon. In each place he assumed that the Church practiced the same sacraments. In each place he assumed that the same doctrine was preached—of Jesus, true God and true man.

Significantly he argues for very little of this. He doesn't even bother to assert it strongly. He assumes it. He mentions it in passing. He can do this because the true Church is universal. That is the literal meaning of the Greek word *katholikos* (catholic). The same term is used in other documents of the second century, and increasingly as time wore on.

The Church is recognizable in every place, not because of a common language or special dress or diet, but because of its doctrine and worship. The proof, St. Ignatius said—and Sts. Polycarp and Irenaeus—is plain to see in the flesh and blood of the Eucharist and in the hierarchy.

> Let no man deceive himself. Both the beings that
> are in heaven, and the glorious angels, and rulers,

---

2   St. Ignatius of Antioch, *Letter to the Ephesians* 18 and *Letter to the Smyrnaeans* 8.

both visible and invisible, if they believe not in the blood of Christ, shall, in consequence, incur condemnation. . . . But consider those who are of a different opinion with respect to the grace of Christ which has come unto us, how opposed they are to the will of God. They have no regard for love; no care for the widow, or the orphan, or the oppressed; of the bond, or of the free; of the hungry, or of the thirsty.

They abstain from the Eucharist and from prayer, because they confess not the Eucharist to be the flesh of our Savior Jesus Christ, which suffered for our sins, and which the Father, of His goodness, raised up again. Those, therefore, who speak against this gift of God, incur death in the midst of their disputes. . . .

See that you all follow the bishop, even as Jesus Christ does the Father, and the presbytery as you would the apostles; and reverence the deacons, as being the institution of God. Let no man do anything connected with the Church without the bishop. Let that be deemed a proper Eucharist, which is administered either by the bishop, or by one to whom he has entrusted it. Wherever the bishop shall appear, there let the multitude also be; even as, wherever Jesus Christ is, there is the Catholic Church.[3]

The catholicity of the Church is necessary for its oneness and its holiness. For, as St. Paul said, God's covenant is no longer applied according to nationality or any other human difference. "There is neither Jew nor Greek, there is neither slave nor free, there is neither male nor female; for you are all one in Christ Jesus" (Gal 3:28). The Church is composed of Israel and everyone else—*all* the Gentile peoples.

Yet catholicity means still more than that. It means more than "worldwide." It means cosmic. Because, as St. Paul noted, the very angels in heaven must receive their doctrine and grace through the Church (see Eph 3:9–10)—the same Church to which Christians on earth belong and in which they meet and worship.

There are *not* multiple churches—one in heaven, one on earth, and one in purgatory. Christians have traditionally believed in one Church that is both heavenly and earthly: a Church that is truly catholic, universal, reaching to the heights of heaven and the plains of earth. To think like a Catholic is to have this sense of the "communion of saints"—both the "saints" in the pews (Col 1:2) and "the saints in light" (Col 1:12).

---

[3] St. Ignatius of Antioch, *Letter to the Smyrnaeans* 6–8.

To know this catholicity is to live life fully in God's covenant family. To be Catholic is never to be alone, always able to go forward in life with hope and confidence.

◆ ◆ ◆

The Church is, finally, apostolic. It is the place where the faith once given to the Apostles is not only preserved, not only protected, but *living*.

In the very passage where St. Paul speaks of our membership in God's covenant family—God's "household"—he says that this household is "built upon the foundation of the apostles and prophets, Christ Jesus himself being the cornerstone" (Eph 2:19–21).

The Apostles are foundational. It is from them, through succession, that all subsequent bishops of the Church have received their authority. It is to their testimony, given in the Scriptures, that the Church in every age is held accountable. "And the wall of the city had twelve foundations, and on them the twelve names of the twelve apostles of the Lamb" (Rev 21:14).

Succession was ensured and established by the practice of the Apostles themselves. They knew they could not be everywhere. They knew they would not live forever. So they established bishops and priests in the places where they founded churches.

The act that ensured succession was sacramental. It was an outward, physical sign that was entrusted to the Church as a means of grace—a "gift of God."

"Do not neglect the gift you have," St. Paul wrote to Timothy, "which was given you by prophetic utterance when the council of elders laid their hands upon you" (1 Tim 4:14). In his next letter, he added, "Hence I remind you to rekindle the gift of God that is within you through the laying on of my hands" (2 Tim 1:6).

Succession has always been an important part of biblical religion. The Old Testament is full of genealogies—royal, priestly, patriarchal, prophetic. Prophecy doesn't end with Elijah's assumption into heaven. It passes to Elisha. The pattern continues in the New Testament, which begins with a genealogy!

Any family identity must account for family origins. In the New Covenant, God's household looks back to Jesus—and, specifically, to his institution of the Church, building it upon the authority of the Apostles.

An apostolic Church is not stationary, however; it is *sent*. That is the root meaning of the word Apostle: one who is sent; an emissary or ambassador. God willed this as the way his Church would be established throughout the earth. He entrusted it to mere mortals—who had hardly proved themselves reliable—and he empowered them sacramentally to act not only in his name, but in his *person*. "He who receives you receives me," he told them, "and he who receives me receives him who sent me" (Mt 10:40). Thus God's omnipotent love infallibly works through fallible sinners to communicate his message of love.

As Jesus sends the Apostles forth, he sends them with the same power with which he himself had been sent. And he envisions a succession of "sendings" into the future, so that the Church may be united in apostolic faith.

> I do not pray for these only, but also for those who believe in me through their word, that they may all be one; even as you, Father, are in me, and I in you, that they also may be in us, so that the world may believe that you have sent me. The glory which thou hast given me I have given to them, that they may be one even as we are one.
>
> — John 17:20–21

♦ ♦ ♦

This is the Church of the saints in "communion." The creed employs the phrase that merely amplifies what it has already affirmed in the confession of the Church as "holy."

The creed, like the New Testament, acknowledges one Baptism (Eph 4:5). And, throughout the first several centuries of Christian history, Baptism was the immediate context for the recitation of the creed. When people recited the creed, they were looking forward to the beginning of a new life in covenant with God—a new life in God's family, the Church.

Beyond this, there was still greater hope. They trusted, upon the testimony of the Church, that their new life would not end. They would live on not only in spirit or in memory, but in the very flesh that God had created for them. They believed in the resurrection of the body and life everlasting.

They believed in the "life of the world to come"—a life in God's kingdom, a kingdom that would "have no end." Yet they were not searching the skies for its arrival. The kingdom had already come with the advent of the King of Kings, Jesus Christ. When he arrived, the kingdom was "at hand" (Mt 3:2). It was imminent. Jesus emphasizes this throughout his ministry (see, for example, Mt 4:17). At the beginning of his Paschal Mystery, as he celebrated the banquet of the New Covenant, he told his Apostles: "I assign to you, as my Father assigned to me, a kingdom" (Lk 22:29). The Greek text literally says: "I covenant to you, as my Father covenanted to me, a kingdom."

The one, holy, catholic, apostolic Church is that kingdom; and we have it, even now, not only by the mechanism of succession, but more importantly by the blood of the covenant. The kingdom has come. It is the Church. It will never end. Not even hell can prevail against it.

That is what we believe and profess when we recite the creed.

CHAPTER 14

AMEN

GREGORY OF NYSSA, both brilliant and holy, was recognized by his contemporaries and peers as a man who most perfectly embodied the Council of Constantinople—the council that produced the creed we call "Nicene" and recite every Sunday. The Emperor Theodosius decreed that communion with Gregory was a necessary condition of orthodoxy. As the council ended, the Fathers appointed Gregory to travel extensively promoting the formulas of the creed in places where controversies had arisen.

While in Constantinople, he complained about the condition of the city's faith. It's not that the people weren't interested, he noted. In fact, they pursued their interest in theology with impressive ardor. Everyone seemed to know the Scriptures and everyone seemed eager to interpret them. But their interpretations veered wildly because the people held themselves accountable to no authority. Gregory complained:

Mere youths and tradesmen are off-hand dogmatists in theology. Servants, too, and slaves that have been flogged . . . are solemn with us and philosophical about things incomprehensible. . . . If you ask for change, someone philosophizes to you on the begotten and the unbegotten. If you ask the price of bread, you're told the Father is greater and the Son inferior. If you ask if the bath is ready, someone answers that the Son was created from nothing.[1]

Gregory's mission was to remedy this situation. His method was the creed.

His mission was needed and essential. If Jesus had wandered into the market and asked his haunting question, "But who do you say that I am?" (Mt 16:15), he would have received many different answers. Most, it seems, would seem quite flattering if applied to mere mortals like you and me, but they would be wrong if applied to God incarnate. And wrong answers about Jesus all come with terrible implications: errors about God, about salvation, and about every dimension of human nature. Christ, after all, is the only one who "fully reveals man to man."[2]

If we don't get the creed right, we don't get Jesus right. And if we don't get him right, we don't get anything right.

---

[1] St. Gregory of Nyssa, *On the Deity of the Son and the Holy Spirit.*

[2] Second Vatican Council, Pastoral Constitution on the Church in the Modern World *Gaudium et Spes*, 22.

Our times are not all that different from Gregory's. If we go to the market, we may encounter many opinions about Jesus—one from the apocalyptic preacher on the street corner, and another from the leaflets left in the laundromat, and still another from the tabloids on sale at the checkout line. Popular books treat Jesus as a guru, psychologist, Republican, Democrat.

In such a climate, what are we, in our turn, to do? Perhaps we should do the same as St. Gregory did, all those years ago. We should go forward, fortified by the creed.

Gregory surely faced resistance because he was presenting something new—a confession of faith that differed markedly from the versions familiar in the churches. In our day we face a different problem: the perception that the creeds are old, tired, worn out, irrelevant, and provincial in their language and concerns. Read the words of the Orthodox scholar Fr. Georges Florovsky, written almost a half-century ago.

> I am fully aware that creeds are a stumbling block for many in our own generation. "The creeds are venerable symbols, like the tattered flags upon the walls of national churches; but for the present warfare of the church in Asia, in Africa, in Europe and America the creeds, when they are understood, are about as serviceable as a battle-ax or an arquebus in the hands of a modern soldier." This was written some years ago by a prominent Brit-

ish scholar who is a devout minister too. . . . But there are still many who would wholeheartedly make this vigorous statement their own.[3]

The creeds have indeed become unfashionable. A hymn popular in liberal Protestant churches, "Praise the Source of Faith and Learning," mocks the very idea of a creed, presenting it as "antiquated" and associating it with "unthinking faith" and even "terror." In the inevitable rhyme for terror, the lyric presents the creed—once the Church's hallmark of truth and the covenant—and presents it as "error."[4] In the 1960s the great French theologian Jean Daniélou, S.J., lamented that already "there is no article of the Creed which is not emptied of its contents by the new sophists, in order to adapt it to the taste of the times."[5]

Yet Daniélou found in the creed "the pure crystalline form and undistorted echo of what I believe." And Florovsky prescribed a simple antidote to modern skepticism and cynicism: "Preach the creeds!" He would preserve the language of the creeds

> not because of a lazy and credulous "conservatism" or a blind "obedience" to some external "au-

---

[3] Georges Florovsky, *Bible, Church, Tradition: An Eastern Orthodox View* (Belmont: Nordland Publishing, 1972), 11.

[4] Thomas H. Troeger, *Praise the Source of Faith and Learning* (New York: Oxford University Press, 1987).

[5] Jean Daniélou, "I Am in the Church," published online at http://www.theveil. net/meta/dan/iam_1.html. Retrieved January 21, 2016.

thorities," but simply because I cannot find any better phraseology. I am prepared to expose myself to the inevitable charge of being "antiquarian" and "fundamentalist." And I would protest that such a charge is gratuitous and wrong. I do keep and hold the "doctrines of the creed," conscientiously and wholeheartedly, because I apprehend by faith their perennial adequacy and relevance to all ages and to all situations, including "a time such as this." And I believe it is precisely the "doctrines of the creed" that can enable a desperate generation like ours to regain Christian courage and vision.[6]

The generation succeeding his "desperate generation" has already grown to adulthood and middle age, but I do not think it has developed a more compelling vision than the one Fr. Florovsky found in the fourth century. In our own time we find courage and vision most compelling among people who cherish the creedal faith. They live not, perhaps, in the divinity schools of the Ivy League, but in lands where Christianity is illegal. There the baptismal confession can still earn a death sentence and people still die for the sake of the creed—for the sake of the covenant.

The creed was created for the sake of the covenant, and the covenant dissolves, conceptually, apart from the

---

[6] Florovsky, 11–12.

creed. No less a theologian than Pope Benedict XVI has described the creed as "the hermeneutic key to the Scriptures, without which any hermeneutic would have to remain silent."[7]

The heretics of the second, third, and fourth centuries made their arguments from Scripture, but they interpreted Scripture by strange lights—new philosophical fashions and academic fads. They made salvation something rational, manageable, and small. They demoted God's fatherhood till it was temporal, comprehensible, and hardly remarkable. They used Scripture, as modern academics use literature, to deconstruct itself. Apart from the confession of God's eternal fatherhood and Christ's eternal sonship, they preached a sterile gospel.

Against such works and pomps the creeds were constructed as bulwarks—as rules and measures of true faith. The pallid heresies faded into nothing, though now and then their ghosts come back to haunt the Church.

But the Church that remains is the Church of the New Covenant—the Church reborn with every Baptism, strengthened with every Eucharist, renewed by every recitation of the creed.

---

[7] Joseph Cardinal Ratzinger, *God's Word: Scripture, Tradition, Office* (San Francisco: Ignatius Press, 2008), 63.

IMPORTANT LATER CREEDS

The Creed of Chalcedon

This confession was adopted in 451 at the Council of Chalcedon.

WE, THEN, FOLLOWING THE HOLY FATHERS, all with one consent, teach men to confess one and the same Son, our Lord Jesus Christ, the same perfect in Godhead and also perfect in manhood; truly God and truly man, of a reasonable [rational] soul and body; consubstantial [coessential] with the Father according to the Godhead, and consubstantial with us according to the Manhood; in all things like unto us, without sin; begotten before all ages of the Father according to the Godhead, and in these latter days, for us and for our salvation, born of the Virgin Mary, the Mother of God, according to the Manhood; one and the same Christ, Son, Lord, only begotten, to be acknowledged in two natures, inconfusedly, unchangeably, indivisibly, inseparably; the distinction of natures being by no means taken away by the union, but rather the property of each nature being preserved, and concurring in one Person and one Subsistence, not parted or divided into two persons, but one and the same Son, and only begotten, God the Word, the Lord Jesus Christ; as the prophets from the beginning [have declared] concerning Him, and the Lord Jesus Christ Himself has taught us, and the Creed of the holy Fathers has handed down to us.

◆ ◆ ◆

Athanasian Creed (*Quicumque Vult*)

The Athanasian Creed was almost certainly not written by St. Athanasius. More likely it was composed in the fifth century. It is clearly in continuity with the great Alexandrian's thought, but considered in light of the later theology of St. Augustine—and applied to the controversies that led to the Council of Chalcedon. The following is based on the translation by Philip Schaff.

WHOSOEVER WILL BE SAVED, before all things it is necessary that he hold the catholic faith. Which faith except every one do keep whole and undefiled; without doubt he shall perish everlastingly. And the catholic faith is this: That we worship one God in Trinity, and Trinity in Unity; neither confounding the Persons; nor dividing the Essence. For there is one Person of the Father; another of the Son; and another of the Holy Ghost. But the Godhead of the Father, of the Son, and of the Holy Ghost, is all one;

the Glory equal, the Majesty coeternal. Such as the Father is; such is the Son; and such is the Holy Ghost. The Father uncreated; the Son uncreated; and the Holy Ghost uncreated. The Father unlimited; the Son unlimited; and the Holy Ghost unlimited. The Father eternal; the Son eternal; and the Holy Ghost eternal. And yet they are not three eternals; but one eternal. As also there are not three uncreated; nor three infinites, but one uncreated; and one infinite. So likewise the Father is Almighty; the Son Almighty; and the Holy Ghost Almighty. And yet they are not three Almighties; but one Almighty. So the Father is God; the Son is God; and the Holy Ghost is God. And yet they are not three Gods; but one God. So likewise the Father is Lord; the Son Lord; and the Holy Ghost Lord. And yet not three Lords; but one Lord. For like as we are compelled by the Christian verity; to acknowledge every Person by himself to be God and Lord; so are we forbidden by the catholic religion to say, there are three Gods, or three Lords. The Father is made of none, neither created, nor begotten. The Son is of the Father alone; not made, nor created; but begotten. The Holy Ghost is of the Father and of the Son; neither made, nor created, nor begotten; but proceeding. So there is one Father, not three Fathers; one Son, not three Sons; one Holy Ghost, not three Holy Ghosts. And in this Trinity none is before, or after another; none is greater, or less than another. But the whole three Persons are coeternal, and coequal. So that in all things, as aforesaid; the Unity in Trinity, and the Trinity in Unity, is to be worshipped. He therefore that will be saved, let him thus think of the Trinity.

Furthermore it is necessary to everlasting salvation; that he also believe faithfully the Incarnation of our Lord Jesus Christ. For the right Faith is, that we believe and confess; that our Lord Jesus Christ, the Son of God, is God and Man; God, of the Essence of the Father; begotten before the worlds; and Man, of the Essence of his Mother, born in the world. Perfect God; and perfect Man, of a reasonable soul and human flesh subsisting. Equal to the Father, as touching his Godhead; and inferior to the Father as touching his Manhood. Who although he is God and Man; yet he is not two, but one Christ. One; not by conversion of the Godhead into flesh; but by assumption of the Manhood by God. One altogether; not by confusion of Essence; but by unity of Person. For as the reasonable soul and flesh is one man; so God and Man is one Christ; Who suffered for our salvation; descended into hell; rose again the third day from the dead. He ascended into heaven, he sits on the right hand of the God the Father Almighty, from whence he will come to judge the living and the dead. At whose coming all men will rise again with their bodies; And shall give account for their own works. And they that have done good shall go into life everlasting; and they that have done evil, into everlasting fire. This is the catholic faith; which except a man believe truly and firmly, he cannot be saved.

◆ ◆ ◆

The Creed of Lateran IV

The Fourth Lateran Council, called in 1215 by Pope Inno-
cent III, was the most important of the Western Medieval
general councils. The Council Fathers promulgated this creed
as their first canon. The following is based on the translation
of H. J. Schroeder.

WE FIRMLY BELIEVE AND OPENLY CONFESS that there is
only one true God, eternal and immense, omnipotent,
unchangeable, incomprehensible, and ineffable, Father,
Son, and Holy Spirit; three Persons indeed but one essence, substance, or nature absolutely simple; the Father
(proceeding) from no one, but the Son from the Father
only, and the Holy Spirit equally from both, always without beginning and end. The Father begetting, the Son
begotten, and the Holy Spirit proceeding; consubstantial and coequal, co-omnipotent, and coeternal, the one
principle of the universe, Creator of all things invisible
and visible, spiritual and corporeal, who from the beginning of time and by His omnipotent power made from
nothing creatures both spiritual and corporeal, angelic,
namely, and mundane, and then human, as it were, common, composed of spirit and body. The devil and the other demons were indeed created by God good by nature
but they became bad through themselves; man, however,
sinned at the suggestion of the devil. This Holy Trinity in

its common essence undivided and in personal properties divided, through Moses, the holy prophets, and other servants gave to the human race at the most opportune intervals of time the doctrine of salvation.

And finally, Jesus Christ, the only begotten Son of God made flesh by the entire Trinity, conceived with the cooperation of the Holy Spirit of Mary ever Virgin, made true man, composed of a rational soul and human flesh, one Person in two natures, pointed out more clearly the way of life. Who according to his divinity is immortal and impassable, according to his humanity was made passable and mortal, suffered on the cross for the salvation of the human race, and being dead descended into hell, rose from the dead, and ascended into heaven. But he descended in soul, arose in flesh, and ascended equally in both; he will come at the end of the world to judge the living and the dead and will render to the reprobate and to the elect according to their works. Who all shall rise with their own bodies which they now have that they may receive according to their merits, whether good or bad, the latter eternal punishment with the devil, the former eternal glory with Christ.

There is one Universal Church of the faithful, outside of which there is absolutely no salvation. In which there is the same priest and sacrifice, Jesus Christ, whose body and blood are truly contained in the sacrament of the altar under the forms of bread and wine; the bread being changed (*transsubstantiatio*) by divine power into the body, and the wine into the blood, so that to realize the mystery of unity we may receive of him what he has received of us. And this sacrament no one can effect except the priest who has been duly ordained in accordance with the keys of the Church, which Jesus Christ himself gave to the Apostles and their successors.

But the sacrament of baptism, which by the invocation of each Person of the Trinity, namely of the Father, Son, and Holy Spirit, is effected in water, duly conferred on children and adults in the form prescribed by the Church by anyone whatsoever, leads to salvation. And should anyone after the reception of baptism have fallen into sin, by true repentance he can always be restored. Not only virgins and those practicing chastity, but also those united in marriage, through the right faith and through works pleasing to God, can merit eternal salvation.

◆ ◆ ◆

The Credo of the People of God
This long profession of faith was promulgated by Pope Blessed Paul VI in his Apostolic Letter Solemni Hac Liturgia, June 30, 1968.

. . . 8. WE BELIEVE IN ONE ONLY GOD, Father, Son and Holy Spirit, creator of things visible such as this world in which our transient life passes, of things invisible such as the pure spirits which are also called angels,(3) and creator in each man of his spiritual and immortal soul.

9. We believe that this only God is absolutely one in His infinitely holy essence as also in all His perfections, in His omnipotence, His infinite knowledge, His providence, His will and His love. He is He who is, as He revealed to Moses;(4) and He is love, as the apostle John teaches us:(5) so that these two names, being and love, express ineffably the same divine reality of Him who has wished to make Himself known to us, and who, "dwelling in light inaccessible,"(6) is in Himself above every name, above every thing and above every created intellect. God alone can give us right and full knowledge of this reality by revealing Himself as Father, Son and Holy Spirit, in whose eternal life we are by grace called to share, here below in the obscurity of faith and after death in eternal light. The mutual bonds which eternally constitute the Three Persons, who are each one and the same divine being, are the blessed inmost life of God thrice holy, infinitely beyond all that we can conceive in human measure.(7) We give thanks, however, to the divine goodness that very many believers can testify with us before men to the unity of God, even though they know not the mystery of the most holy Trinity.

The Father
10. We believe then in the Father who eternally begets the Son; in the Son, the Word of God, who is eternally begotten; in the Holy Spirit, the uncreated Person who

proceeds from the Father and the Son as their eternal love. Thus in the Three Divine Persons, *coaeternae sibi et coaequales*,(8) the life and beatitude of God perfectly one superabound and are consummated in the supreme excellence and glory proper to uncreated being, and always "there should be venerated unity in the Trinity and Trinity in the unity."(9)

The Son

11. We believe in our Lord Jesus Christ, who is the Son of God. He is the Eternal Word, born of the Father before time began, and one in substance with the Father, *homoousios to Patri*,(10) and through Him all things were made. He was incarnate of the Virgin Mary by the power of the Holy Spirit, and was made man: equal therefore to the Father according to His divinity, and inferior to the Father according to His humanity;(11) and Himself one, not by some impossible confusion of His natures, but by the unity of His person. (12)

12. He dwelt among us, full of grace and truth. He proclaimed and established the Kingdom of God and made us know in Himself the Father. He gave us His new commandment to love one another as He loved us. He taught us the way of the beatitudes of the Gospel: poverty in spirit, meekness, suffering borne with patience, thirst after justice, mercy, purity of heart, will for peace, persecution suffered for justice sake. Under Pontius Pilate He suffered—the Lamb of God bearing on Himself the sins

of the world, and He died for us on the cross, saving us by His redeeming blood. He was buried, and, of His own power, rose on the third day, raising us by His resurrection to that sharing in the divine life which is the life of grace. He ascended to heaven, and He will come again, this time in glory, to judge the living and the dead: each according to his merits—those who have responded to the love and piety of God going to eternal life, those who have refused them to the end going to the fire that is not extinguished.

And His Kingdom will have no end.

The Holy Spirit

13. We believe in the Holy Spirit, who is Lord and Giver of life, who is adored and glorified together with the Father and the Son. He spoke to us by the prophets; He was sent by Christ after His resurrection and His ascension to the Father; He illuminates, vivifies, protects and guides the Church; He purifies the Church's members if they do not shun His grace. His action, which penetrates to the inmost of the soul, enables man to respond to the call of Jesus: Be perfect as your Heavenly Father is perfect (Mt. 5:48).

14. We believe that Mary is the Mother, who remained ever a Virgin, of the Incarnate Word, our God and Savior Jesus Christ,(13) and that by reason of this singular election, she was, in consideration of the merits of her Son, redeemed in a more eminent manner,(14) preserved

from all stain of original sin(15) and filled with the gift of grace more than all other creatures.(16)

15. Joined by a close and indissoluble bond to the Mysteries of the Incarnation and Redemption,(17) the Blessed Virgin, the Immaculate, was at the end of her earthly life raised body and soul to heavenly glory(18) and likened to her risen Son in anticipation of the future lot of all the just; and we believe that the Blessed Mother of God, the New Eve, Mother of the Church,(19) continues in heaven her maternal role with regard to Christ's members, cooperating with the birth and growth of divine life in the souls of the redeemed.(20)

Original Offense

16. We believe that in Adam all have sinned, which means that the original offense committed by him caused human nature, common to all men, to fall to a state in which it bears the consequences of that offense, and which is not the state in which it was at first in our first parents— established as they were in holiness and justice, and in which man knew neither evil nor death. It is human nature so fallen, stripped of the grace that clothed it, injured in its own natural powers and subjected to the dominion of death, that is transmitted to all men, and it is in this sense that every man is born in sin. We therefore hold, with the Council of Trent, that original sin is transmitted with human nature, "not by imitation, but by propagation" and that it is thus "proper to everyone."(21)

Reborn of the Holy Spirit

17. We believe that our Lord Jesus Christ, by the sacrifice of the cross redeemed us from original sin and all the personal sins committed by each one of us, so that, in accordance with the word of the apostle, "where sin abounded, grace did more abound."(22)

Baptism

18. We believe in one Baptism instituted by our Lord Jesus Christ for the remission of sins. Baptism should be administered even to little children who have not yet been able to be guilty of any personal sin, in order that, though born deprived of supernatural grace, they may be reborn "of water and the Holy Spirit" to the divine life in Christ Jesus.(23)

The Church

19. We believe in one, holy, catholic, and apostolic Church, built by Jesus Christ on that rock which is Peter. She is the Mystical Body of Christ; at the same time a visible society instituted with hierarchical organs, and a spiritual community; the Church on earth, the pilgrim People of God here below, and the Church filled with heavenly blessings; the germ and the first fruits of the Kingdom of God, through which the work and the sufferings of Redemption are continued throughout human history, and which looks for its perfect accomplishment beyond time in glory.(24) In the course of time, the Lord Jesus forms

His Church by means of the sacraments emanating from His plenitude.(25) By these she makes her members participants in the Mystery of the Death and Resurrection of Christ, in the grace of the Holy Spirit who gives her life and movement.(26) She is therefore holy, though she has sinners in her bosom, because she herself has no other life but that of grace: it is by living by her life that her members are sanctified; it is by removing themselves from her life that they fall into sins and disorders that prevent the radiation of her sanctity. This is why she suffers and does penance for these offenses, of which she has the power to heal her children through the blood of Christ and the gift of the Holy Spirit.

The Word

20. Heiress of the divine promises and daughter of Abraham according to the Spirit, through that Israel whose scriptures she lovingly guards, and whose patriarchs and prophets she venerates; founded upon the apostles and handing on from century to century their ever-living word and their powers as pastors in the successor of Peter and the bishops in communion with him; perpetually assisted by the Holy Spirit, she has the charge of guarding, teaching, explaining and spreading the Truth which God revealed in a then veiled manner by the prophets, and fully by the Lord Jesus. We believe all that is contained in the word of God written or handed down, and that the Church proposes for belief as divinely revealed, whether

by a solemn judgment or by the ordinary and universal magisterium.(27) We believe in the infallibility enjoyed by the successor of Peter when he teaches ex cathedra as pastor and teacher of all the faithful,(28) and which is assured also to the episcopal body when it exercises with him the supreme magisterium.(29)

21. We believe that the Church founded by Jesus Christ and for which He prayed is indefectibly one in faith, worship and the bond of hierarchical communion. In the bosom of this Church, the rich variety of liturgical rites and the legitimate diversity of theological and spiritual heritages and special disciplines, far from injuring her unity, make it more manifest.(30)

One Shepherd

22. Recognizing also the existence, outside the organism of the Church of Christ, of numerous elements of truth and sanctification which belong to her as her own and tend to Catholic unity,(31) and believing in the action of the Holy Spirit who stirs up in the heart of the disciples of Christ love of this unity,(32) we entertain the hope that the Christians who are not yet in the full communion of the one only Church will one day be reunited in one flock with one only shepherd.

23. We believe that the Church is necessary for salvation, because Christ, who is the sole mediator and way of salvation, renders Himself present for us in His body which is the Church.(33) But the divine design of

salvation embraces all men; and those who without fault on their part do not know the Gospel of Christ and His Church, but seek God sincerely, and under the influence of grace endeavor to do His will as recognized through the promptings of their conscience, they, in a number known only to God, can obtain salvation.(34)

Sacrifice of Calvary

24. We believe that the Mass, celebrated by the priest representing the person of Christ by virtue of the power received through the Sacrament of Orders, and offered by him in the name of Christ and the members of His Mystical Body, is the sacrifice of Calvary rendered sacramentally present on our altars. We believe that as the bread and wine consecrated by the Lord at the Last Supper were changed into His body and His blood which were to be offered for us on the cross, likewise the bread and wine consecrated by the priest are changed into the body and blood of Christ enthroned gloriously in heaven, and we believe that the mysterious presence of the Lord, under what continues to appear to our senses as before, is a true, real and substantial presence.(35)

Transubstantiation

25. Christ cannot be thus present in this sacrament except by the change into His body of the reality itself of the bread and the change into His blood of the reality itself of the wine, leaving unchanged only the properties of the

bread and wine which our senses perceive. This mysterious change is very appropriately called by the Church transubstantiation. Every theological explanation which seeks some understanding of this mystery must, in order to be in accord with Catholic faith, maintain that in the reality itself, independently of our mind, the bread and wine have ceased to exist after the Consecration, so that it is the adorable body and blood of the Lord Jesus that from then on are really before us under the sacramental species of bread and wine,(36) as the Lord willed it, in order to give Himself to us as food and to associate us with the unity of His Mystical Body.(37)

26. The unique and indivisible existence of the Lord glorious in heaven is not multiplied, but is rendered present by the sacrament in the many places on earth where Mass is celebrated. And this existence remains present, after the sacrifice, in the Blessed Sacrament which is, in the tabernacle, the living heart of each of our churches. And it is our very sweet duty to honor and adore in the blessed Host which our eyes see, the Incarnate Word whom they cannot see, and who, without leaving heaven, is made present before us.

Temporal Concern

27. We confess that the Kingdom of God begun here below in the Church of Christ is not of this world whose form is passing, and that its proper growth cannot be confounded with the progress of civilization, of science

or of human technology, but that it consists in an ever more profound knowledge of the unfathomable riches of Christ, an ever stronger hope in eternal blessings, an ever more ardent response to the love of God, and an ever more generous bestowal of grace and holiness among men. But it is this same love which induces the Church to concern herself constantly about the true temporal welfare of men. Without ceasing to recall to her children that they have not here a lasting dwelling, she also urges them to contribute, each according to his vocation and his means, to the welfare of their earthly city, to promote justice, peace and brotherhood among men, to give their aid freely to their brothers, especially to the poorest and most unfortunate. The deep solicitude of the Church, the Spouse of Christ, for the needs of men, for their joys and hopes, their griefs and efforts, is therefore nothing other than her great desire to be present to them, in order to illuminate them with the light of Christ and to gather them all in Him, their only Savior. This solicitude can never mean that the Church conform herself to the things of this world, or that she lessen the ardor of her expectation of her Lord and of the eternal Kingdom.

28. We believe in the life eternal. We believe that the souls of all those who die in the grace of Christ whether they must still be purified in purgatory, or whether from the moment they leave their bodies Jesus takes them to paradise as He did for the Good Thief are the People of God in the eternity beyond death, which will be finally conquered on

the day of the Resurrection when these souls will be reunited with their bodies.

Prospect of Resurrection

29. We believe that the multitude of those gathered around Jesus and Mary in paradise forms the Church of Heaven where in eternal beatitude they see God as He is,(38) and where they also, in different degrees, are associated with the holy angels in the divine rule exercised by Christ in glory, interceding for us and helping our weakness by their brotherly care.(39)

30. We believe in the communion of all the faithful of Christ, those who are pilgrims on earth, the dead who are attaining their purification, and the blessed in heaven, all together forming one Church; and we believe that in this communion the merciful love of God and His saints is ever listening to our prayers, as Jesus told us: Ask and you will receive.(40) Thus it is with faith and in hope that we look forward to the resurrection of the dead, and the life of the world to come.

Blessed be God Thrice Holy. Amen.

3.   Cf. Dz.-Sch. 3002.
4.   Cf. Ex. 3:14.
5.   Cf. 1 Jn. 4:8.
6.   Cf. 1 Tim. 6:16.
7.   Cf. Dz.-Sch. 804.

8. Cf. Dz.-Sch. 75.
9. Cf. ibid.
10. Cf. Dz.-Sch. 150.
11. Cf. Dz.-Sch. 76.
12. Cf. ibid.
13. Cf. Dz.-Sch. 251-252.
14. Cf. *Lumen Gentium*, 53.
15. Cf. Dz.-Sch. 2803.
16. Cf. *Lumen Gentium*, 53.
17. Cf. *Lumen Gentium*, 53, 58, 61.
18. Cf. Dz.-Sch. 3903.
19. Cf. *Lumen Gentium*, 53, 56, 61, 63; cf. Paul VI, *Alloc. for the Closing of the Third Session of the Second Vatican Council*: A.A.S. LVI [1964] 1016; cf. Exhort. Apost. *Signum Magnum*, Introd.
20. Cf. *Lumen Gentium*, 62; cf. Paul VI, Exhort. Apost. *Signum Magnum*, p. 1, n. 1.
21. Cf. Dz.-Sch. 1513.
22. Cf. Rom. 5:20.
23. Cf. Dz.-Sch. 1514.
24. Cf. *Lumen Gentium*, 8, 5.
25. Cf. *Lumen Gentium*, 7, 11.
26. Cf. *Sacrosanctum Concilium*, 5, 6; cf. *Lumen Gentium*, 7, 12, 50.
27. Cf. Dz.-Sch. 3011.
28. Cf. Dz.-Sch. 3074.
29. Cf. *Lumen Gentium*, 25.
30. Cf. *Lumen Gentium*, 23; cf. *Orientalium Ecclesiarum* 2, 3, 5, 6.
31. Cf. *Lumen Gentium*, 8.
32. Cf. *Lumen Gentium*, 15.
33. Cf. *Lumen Gentium*, 14.
34. Cf. *Lumen Gentium*, 16.
35. Cf. Dz.-Sch. 1651.
36. Cf. Dz.-Sch. 1642, 1651–1654; Paul VI, Enc. *Mysterium Fidei*.
37. Cf. S. Th., 111, 73, 3.
38. Cf. 1 Jn. 3:2; Dz.-Sch. 1000.
39. Cf. *Lumen Gentium*, 49.
40. Cf. Lk. 10:9–10; Jn. 16:24.

A BIBLICAL CREED

THE NICENE CREED, with references to scriptural sources.

I believe in one God, (Deut 6:4; Mk 12:29, 32)
the Father (Mt 5:48, 6:9; Mk 14:36; Lk 23:46; Jn 5:18)
Almighty, (Job 37:23; Mt 26:64)
Maker of heaven and earth, (Gen 1:1; 14:9; Acts 4:24;
     Rev 10:6)
of all things visible and invisible. (Col 1:16)

I believe in one Lord Jesus Christ, (Acts 2:36, 15:11,
     16:31; Rom 5:1; 1 Thess 5:28; 2 Thess 3:18)
the Only Begotten Son of God, (Jn 1:14, 18; 3:16, 18)
born of the Father before all ages. (Lk 1:35; Jn 1:1–3)
God from God, Light from Light, true God from true
God, begotten, not made, consubstantial with the Father,
     (Heb 1:3)
Through Him all things were made. (Heb 1:3)
For us men and for our salvation He came down from
     heaven, (Jn 3:13)

and by the Holy Spirit was incarnate of the Virgin Mary,
and became man. (Mt 1:18–25; Lk 1:35)

For our sake He was crucified under Pontius Pilate, (Mt
27:26; Mk 15:15; Lk 23:24; Jn 19:16)

He suffered death and was buried, and rose again on the
third day in accordance with the Scriptures.
(1 Cor 15:3–4)

He ascended into heaven (Lk 24:51; Acts 1:9–10)
and is seated at the right hand of the Father. (Mk
16:19; Col 3:1)

He will come again in glory to judge the living and the
dead (Rom14:9; 2 Tim 4:1)

and His kingdom will have no end. (Lk 1:33)

I believe in the Holy Spirit, the Lord, the Giver of life,
(Jn 14:26; 16:7–11; Acts 2:17; 2 Cor 3:6)

who proceeds from the Father and the Son, who with
the Father and the Son is adored and glorified, (Jn
14:16; Rom 16:27; 2 Tim 4:18)

who has spoken through the prophets. (Heb 1:1;
1 Pet 1:10–11)

I believe in One, (Jn 17:21; Rom 12:5)
Holy, (John 17:17,19; Eph 5:25–27)
Catholic, (Mt 28:19)
and Apostolic Church. (Mt 28:20)

I confess one baptism for the forgiveness of sins
  (Acts 2:38; 22:16)
and I look forward the resurrection of the dead (Acts
  24:15; Rom 6:5; 2 Cor 4:14)
and the life of the world to come. (Jn 3:16; 5:29;
  Jude 1:21)

Amen. (Ps 106:48; 2 Cor 1:20)

SELECTED BIBLIOGRAPHY

Anatolios, Khaled. *Retrieving Nicaea: The Development and Meaning of Trinitarian Doctrine*. Grand Rapids: Baker, 2011.

Ayo, Nicholas. *Creed as Symbol*. Notre Dame: University of Notre Dame Press, 2004.

Ayres, Lewis. *Nicaea and Its Legacy: An Approach to Fourth-Century Trinitarian Theology*. New York: Oxford University Press, 2006.

Barth, Karl. *Credo*. New York: Charles Scribner's Sons, 1962.

Behr, John. *The Way to Nicaea*. Crestwood: Saint Vladimir's Seminary Press, 2001.

Bezançon, Jean-Noël, Philippe Ferlay, and Jean-Marie Onfray. *How to Understand the Creed* [*Pour Dire le Credo*]. Translated by John Bowden. London: SCM Press Ltd., 1987.

Briggs, Charles Augustus. *Theological Symbolics*. International Theological Library. New York: Charles Scribner's Sons, 1914.

Claudel, Paul. *I Believe in God: A Meditation on the Apostles' Creed*. Edited by Agnès du Sarment. Translated by Helen Weaver. Introduction by Henri de Lubac, S.J. New York: Holt, Rinehart and Winston, Inc., 1963.

Confessing the One Faith: An Ecumenical Explication of the Apostolic Faith as it is Confessed in the Nicene-Constantinopolitan Creed (381), Faith and Order Paper no. 153. Geneva, Switzerland: WCC Publications, 1992.

Crean, Thomas. *The Mass and the Saints.* San Francisco: Ignatius Press, 2009.

Crehan, Joseph. *Early Christian Baptism and the Creed: A Study In Ante-Nicene Theology.* London: Burns, Oates, & Washbourne Ltd., 1950.

De Lubac, Henri. *The Christian Faith.* San Francisco: Ignatius Press, 1986.

Ferguson, Everett. *The Rule of Faith: A Guide.* Eugene: Cascade, 2015.

George, Timothy, ed. *Evangelicals and the Nicene Faith: Reclaiming the Apostolic Witness.* Grand Rapids: Baker Academic, 2011.

Hahn, Scott. *A Father Who Keeps His Promises: God's Covenant Love in Scripture.* Ann Arbor: Servant, 1998.

———. *Swear to God: The Promise and Power of the Sacraments.* New York: Doubleday, 2004.

Harmless, William. *Augustine and the Catechumenate.* Collegeville: The Liturgical Press, 1995.

Hill, Wesley. *Paul and the Trinity: Persons, Relations, and the Pauline Letters.* Grand Rapids: Eerdmans, 2015.

Hinlicky, Paul R. *Divine Complexity: The Rise of Creedal Christianity.* Minneapolis: Fortress Press, 2011.

Hogan, Richard M. *Dissent from the Creed: Heresies Past and Present*. Huntington: Our Sunday Visitor, 2001.

Horton, Michael. *We Believe: Recovering the Essentials of the Apostles' Creed*. Nashville: Word Publishing, 1998.

Jenson, Robert W. *Canon and Creed*. Louisville: Westminster John Knox Press, 2010.

Johnson, Luke Timothy. *The Creed: What Christians Believe and Why it Matters*. New York: Doubleday, 2005.

Kelly, J. N. D. *Early Christian Creeds*. London: Longmans, Green and Co. Ltd, 1950.

Kemmer, Alfons. *The Creed in the Gospels: An Introduction to the Biblical Sources of the Creed* [*Das Glaubensbekenntnis in den Evangelien*]. Translated by Urban Schnaus, O.S.B. New York: Paulist Press, 1986.

Kline, Meredith G. *By Oath Consigned: A Reinterpretation of the Covenant Signs of Circumcision and Baptism*. Grand Rapids: Eerdmans, 1968.

Knox, Ronald. *The Creed in Slow Motion*. New York: Sheed and Ward, 1949.

Lias, J. J. *The Nicene Creed: A Manual for the Use of Candidates for Holy Orders*. New York: The Macmillan Co., 1897.

Lienhard, Joseph T., and Frédéric Curnier-Laroche. *Splendors of the Creed*. Yonkers: Magnificat, 2013.

Mazza, Enrico. *Mystagogy: A Theology of Liturgy in the Patristic Age*. New York: Pueblo, 1989.

Neufeld, Vernon H. *The Earliest Christian Confessions*. Grand Rapids: Eerdmans, 1963.

Norris, Richard A., ed. and trans. *The Christological Controversy*. Philadelphia: Fortress, 1980.

Pelikan, Jaroslav. *Credo: Historical and Theological Guide to Creeds and Confessions of Faith in the Christian Tradition*. New Haven: Yale University Press, 2005.

———, and Valerie Hotchkiss, eds. *Creeds and Confessions of Faith in the Christian Tradition*. 4 vols. New Haven: Yale University Press, 2003.

Pietras, Henryk. *Council of Nicaea (325): Religious and Political Context, Documents, Commentaries*. Rome: Gregorian & Biblical Press, 2016.

Quick, Oliver Chase. *Doctrines of the Creed: Their Basis in Scripture and Their Meaning Today*. London: Nisbet & Co. Ltd., 1947.

Radner, Ephraim, and George Sumner, eds. *The Rule of Faith: Scripture, Canon, and Creed in a Critical Age*. Harrisburg: Morehouse Publishing, 1998.

Ratzinger, Cardinal Joseph. *The God of Jesus Christ: Meditations on the Triune God*. San Francisco: Ignatius Press, 2008.

———. *Introduction to Christianity*. San Francisco: Ignatius Press, 2008.

——— (Benedict XVI). *I Believe in One God: The Creed Explained*. Edited by Giuliano Vigini. Foreword by Cardinal Timothy Dolan. New York: St. Paul's Publishing, 2012.

Ray, Stephen K., and R. Dennis Walters. *The Faith for Beginners: Understanding the Creeds*. San Diego: Catholic Answers: 2006.

Rusch, William G., ed. and trans. *The Trinitarian Controversy*. Philadelphia: Fortress, 1980.

Sayers, Dorothy L. *Creed or Chaos? And Other Essays in Popular Theology*. London: Methuen & Co. Ltd., 1954.

Scheeben, M. J. *The Mysteries of Christianity*. St. Louis: Herder, 1946.

Schönborn, Cardinal Christoph. *God Sent His Son: A Contemporary Christology*. San Francisco: Ignatius Press, 2010.

Seitz, Christopher R., ed. *Nicene Christianity: The Future for a New Ecumenism*. Grand Rapids: Brazos Press, 2001.

Shamon, Albert J. *Treasure Untold: Reflections on The Apostles' Creed*. Westminster, Maryland: The Newman Press, 1955.

Skilton, John H. *Scripture and Confession: A Book About Confessions Old and New*. Nutley, New Jersey: Presbyterian and Reformed Publishing Co., 1973.

Stevenson, J. Revised by W. H. C. Frend. *Creeds, Councils, and Controversies: Documents Illustrating the History of the Church AD 337–461*. London: SPCK, 1989.

Tanner, Norman F. *Decrees of the Ecumenical Councils*. 2 vols. Washington, DC: Georgetown University Press, 1990.

Weinandy, Thomas. *The Father's Spirit of Sonship: Reconceiving the Trinity*. London: T. & T. Clark, 1995.

Wuerl, Cardinal Donald. *Faith That Transforms Us: Reflections on the Creed*. Frederick: Word Among Us, 2013.